Your review supports our mission of inspiring happy, magnetic homes and lives for everyone. Please leave an honest review on Amazon.

Just scan the QR code with your phone's camera and leave a review. Thank you.

Take Before Photos! You will be glad you did!

So many times my clients wish they had before and after photos of the visible changes they make. Take photos of every room in the house, your garage and the front of your house. Not only will you feel your energy change, you will be able to see the changes.

If you upload before and after photos with your Amazon review or send me an email to hello@tonja.com with before and after's included, I will gift you with a 30-minute Magnetic Home consultation.

Tonja

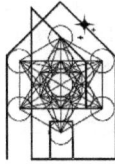

To order copies in quantities contact Tonja Waring at 972.632.6364

ISBN--13: 978-1944913-72-4

ISBN-10: 978-1944913-73-1

TABLE OF CONTENTS

TABLE OF CONTENTS

MAGNETIC HOME

TONJA WARING

INTRODUCTION

This is not just a book. **It's an energy reset, a sacred guide, and a powerful tool** for anyone ready to create a home that supports their health and wealth and brings positive experiences to their life and those who they invite to share in the experience of their home.

If you're here to live on purpose, raise your frequency, and attract your most magical life yet – start with your space and I will show you how step-by-step, layer-by-layer.

You are the energy.
Your home is the amplifier.
Let's turn it up!

It all starts with getting crystal clear (and staying clear) about what you want and tuning your frequency and the frequency of your space to such a level that you can't help but get what you want – and you get to have so much fun doing it!

It's like a game and
every day you hit the jackpot!

We are manifesting all the time – every moment, every breath, every thought. What you have been experiencing in life is a reflection of your personal energetic vibration. Most people don't realize that they are sending signals to the Universe all the time - good and not so good - it's automatic.

Your home is sending signals, too.

Whether it's a cluttered corner, a dead plant, a broken drawer, or a room you never use -- your space holds energy, intention, and stories. And that energy is either amplifying your dreams... or slowing them down.

Magnetic Home is more than interior design; it is about intentionally using your energy to leave an imprint on your home that sends a signal to the Quantum Field to get you from where you are now to where you want to be eighteen months from today.

Imagine if your life went off automatic pilot and suddenly you became aware of the signals you are really sending out to the Universe through your beliefs and your home. What is possible for you then? It's exciting to think about.

Sadly, 92% of people never achieve their goals.

Magnetic Home is a tool to help you create the life you have been wanting and deserve to have.

I've taught hundreds of clients how to change their lives – by changing the energy in their minds, their bodies, their homes and their offices.

Afterall, your space reflects your life.

By moving things around at home with your most powerful tool – your simple intention - you can create a higher vibration that draws to you what you want rather than pushing it away from you. When your space matches your vision, good things start happening more frequently. That's when you start spiraling up and get in the flow of success.

This book is for homemakers, business owners, energy healers, and anyone who is waking up spiritually and ready to live their life on purpose and use their energetic presence and mindfulness to turn their space into a sacred co-creator.

Together, we'll walk through:

- ✓ How energy moves through your home (and your life)
- ✓ How to shift what's stuck, stagnant, or out of alignment
- ✓ How to use frequencies, Manifesting Feng Shui, and sacred intention to power up your magnetic flow

✓ And how to turn your everyday spaces into portals of abundance, peace, and power

Through this journey of creating a Magnetic Home, you'll learn powerful Manifesting Feng Shui principles, sacred rituals, and get into the kind of action that moves your energy flow in the best direction. Whether it's your office, garden, bedroom, or bathroom, every part of your space is ready and waiting to support your highest life.

Are you excited to get started? Let's go!

Chapter 1

Get Your Energy Flowing

There are a couple ways you can use this book. You can learn a few principles in the Quick Start Guide and start making adjustments within a few minutes, having loads of fun and freeing up some stagnant energy. (I highly recommend this for everyone.)

Or you can read and study the principles in depth and learn all kinds of ways to create an incredible energy vortex that supports all of your dreams and desires before you do *too much* (if there is such a thing.)

Or you could open up to your Higher Self and randomly open the book to any page trusting that what you read is the perfect place to start for you. That's right, just close your eyes and flip to a page and see what the Universe has in store.

The point is that there is no right or wrong way to use this book.

Either way, it's going to be practical, useful and powerful. Creating your Magnetic Home can be a "one and done" experience, or like personal growth and development, it can be a lifelong adventure! Choose the lifelong adventure!

I'm not always moving things around my house, but I do check in with myself daily through journaling to get a better idea of what I want and what I can do to bring my dreams and goals to fruition. Just now, I moved my desk to face another direction that felt better for what I'm doing. Start checking in with yourself. Do I feel better sitting here? Or here? You can feel a difference. One of the most important areas of the home is where you sleep. So, let's make sure that it is working for you. One-third of your life is sleeping and recharging. Getting that working for you makes the other two-thirds so much better!

In 1999 I graduated with advanced feng shui studies from The Wind and Water School of Feng Shui taught by Carole Hyder. In 2010, I completed my year-long Law of Attraction Coaching Certification at the Quantum Coaching Academy taught by Christy Whitman. Each of these courses have been instrumental in how I respond to the magic and curve balls life sends my way.

I have taught myself how to tune out what I think I should be doing or what others will approve of me doing and tune into what I want, what I really have a desire to do if no one were judging. One Abraham Hicks lesson I learned early on and it plays loudly in my mind on repeat.

"There is never a crowd on the leading edge."

~Abraham Hicks

You were born with your own unique path. That path comes with ups and downs. Here, you have ways to take advantage of both. Some of the methods I teach are my own, but most are a conglomeration of principles that I have learned from master teachers through various workshops and certifications. Largely, my teachings are that of ancient wisdom and some are just good old common sense.

What is Manifesting Feng Shui?

To *manifest* means to bring something into existence or reality through thought and belief. *Feng shui* is a 3,000–5,000-year-old Chinese art and science that uses a nine-life-area *bagua* as a map, overlaying it onto any space – your home, office, bedroom, even your desktop. This map reveals what's happening in the lives of the people who occupy that space.

Manifesting Feng Shui is using the principles of manifesting and feng shui to align the energy of your mind, heart and home for exponential results.

I've used Manifesting Feng Shui to call in my dream home more than once. When I became an empty-nester, I manifested a travel company that allowed me to meet amazing new friends and explore 15 countries across six continents in just the last two years – a vision I first saw in my bathroom seven years earlier.

That is not a coincidence.

That is the power of creating a Magnetic Home that inspires you to live your best life! It speaks to you, supports you and through intention and the alignment of heart, mind and home, you can create this wherever you may travel in the world.

My desire is to share this wisdom with the intent that it be world-changing and everlasting, even if it means transforming one person/one home/one office at a time. I'm happy you feel inclined to create a Magnetic Home and putting your intentions out into the Universe may just be exactly what brought you here.

First and foremost, start having fun with this!

You could even make yourself a magic wand and tap things as you change them for extra energy. Dance around and sing as you move your stuff. Take a shower or bath, put on your favorite outfit just for the occasion of making these life-changing adjustments. Smile big and come from the highest energy place you can as you are working with your home; it matters!

You don't have to believe everything you are doing
to have miracles in your life.

I have made many adjustments I thought were a bit crazy and you know what? Those were some of the adjustments that worked the best for me and my clients. You can fix and refine any adjustments you make. Magnetic Homes are created with layers of intention, and everything is always changing, ever moving. That's energy and you get to stay in the flow.

Quick Start Guide

Be Clear on What You Want

When you picked up this book, what was tugging at your heart? Was there something special you wanted to manifest – or perhaps something about your home you're ready to shift?

- ✓ Maybe you'd love to clear some clutter.
- ✓ Maybe you're ready to call in a promotion.
- ✓ Maybe you want to feel vibrant health again.

Whatever it is, there is magic and power in knowing what you want most. I've always said, "Clarity is the seed to prosperity." And prosperity isn't just about money. It's about a life well lived, feeling abundant in relationships, health and harmony.

exercise

Take a breath. Tune in. Then, quickly jot down a list of the things you'd love to improve in your current situation. Don't censor yourself. Don't overthink. Just write. Take 10 minutes. (I left a few pages blank in the back of the chapter if you need a quick place to write.)

- ✓ Once you have your list, circle three to five things that feel most important right now.

- ✓ Then put a big star next to the one that lights you up the most - the one that, if you could snap your fingers and make it appear, would make you smile inside and out with the enthusiasm of a three-year-old at the best birthday party ever!

8

Here's something important to remember: we can't manifest by trying to change someone else. That's their journey. But what is meant for you will come to you.

Here's a little example of what I'm talking about. Let's say that you want Harry to bring you flowers. Instead of writing, *"I want Harry to bring me flowers,"* bring the focus back to YOU. If flowers lift your spirits and you think you can only have them if they are given to you, release that idea. Next time you see flowers, buy them for yourself and let them fill your space with beauty.

Now, if buying them only makes you resentful because you can't get over wishing Harry was bringing you flowers... then skip it. You get my drift? Only do what makes you feel good or reminds you of something that makes you feel good. Manifesting works best when your energy is lit up, playful, and aligned with joy. That's the frequency where miracles happen.

Write Your Intentions in a Positive Way

Here is another example. Rather than say, "I don't want all this debt." It is more powerful to think and talk about *increasing your savings*. What we focus on expands and all too often, if the conversation in your head plays like a bad record *about reducing debt*, you subconsciously are contributing to your feeling of being in debt or not having enough money. This keeps you stuck in this pattern. The conversation about debt is prolific in our society. It takes conscious effort to break this pattern.

Only you can shift your "fear/frustration" of where you are to "focus" on where you want to be. It's a muscle that we get to develop within ourselves like going to the gym. It takes mastery.

Having a savings account that makes you feel at ease is the difference between 10% of your thoughts and energy being consumed by money and 90% of your thoughts and energy being consumed by money when you don't feel you have enough. Imagine what you could do with all that extra energy if you focus on and play a game to grow your savings account!

Having a nest egg to cover our essential needs puts us at ease; we feel more relaxed, and money starts flowing to us more easily and effortlessly because our vibration is higher.

Connect with Your Home.

When you are working with your home, room, office or any space, be mindful of your intention as you make the changes. Connect with the energy around you. You can simply close your eyes and open your heart to connect energetically, saying a prayer of gratitude for being there. You can state your intention silently or out loud with your hands on your heart.

Or you can take it a step further and create an altar with offerings of flowers, burn incense or a candle and/or write your intentions on a piece of pretty paper. Red is an auspicious color so you can use red ink, a red candle or red paper if you have it. Let your creative intuition guide you. This is your process.

Feel gratitude for your home for all that it has provided for you and will continue to provide for you while you live there. You can also ask if there is anything you should know. You may or may not experience a message through sound, visual imagery or a single word. When you feel you are complete, open your eyes and look around. Make some notes of anything that pops out at you. It's helpful to write today's date at the top of your paper so you can keep a record of what you do and record your successes.

Take a Home Inventory

Begin by standing with your back to the front door, looking into your home. Ask yourself, *"How does this feel to me?"* Even better, step outside, walk a few paces away, and then turn around. Notice what it feels like to approach your home and walk back inside. Make a few mental notes about what you sense or what you'd like to change.

Once inside, pause for a deep breath. Center yourself. Relax. You may even want to close your eyes for a moment to tune into the energy of your space. Notice your thoughts, images, or feelings. Allow yourself to simply feel what you feel. When you're ready, open your eyes and take in your surroundings.

Ask yourself:

- Do I like the way my home feels when I enter?
- Does my home give me energy, or does it take energy from me?
- Do I feel overwhelmed with things to do, or do I feel supported and at peace here?

Remember, this isn't about creating a picture-perfect showcase home. Overly meticulous homes can feel sterile, while homes with clutter can sometimes feel cozy and welcoming. You'll learn more about these dynamics as you continue reading.

Now, describe your overall feeling in one or two sentences.

Next, rate how you feel about your home on a scale of 1 to 10:

$$1 - 2 - 3 - 4 - 5 - 6 - 7 - 8 - 9 - 10$$

From your observations, write down a few specific things you'd like to change.

If you notice many things, don't worry – you don't have to change everything overnight. Shifting a home's energy too quickly can sometimes feel overwhelming or chaotic. Small, intentional changes create magnetic momentum. If you see just a few things you're eager to shift, let your excitement guide you and begin there.

Using subtle ways to move energy can produce powerful results. That is why intention is most important. A small change like sweeping your front step with the intention of bringing positive energy to your home can give you the experience of having more energy and feeling lighter. The cures and adjustments with Manifesting Feng Shui are seldom expensive for this reason.

I recently met with a client who told me she was satisfied with the furniture in her home. I really felt she was lying to herself, and I told her so, gently of course. In a two-minute conversation, she gave herself permission to design her home in a way she loves and feels good about.

In her industry she has outproduced her colleagues 4 to 1 with little recognition or financial compensation. Interestingly, we found her diploma from an Ivy League school where she graduated with honors on the bottom of her closet. She took her diploma to her office and hung it on the wall behind her with two other framed awards. Within only a couple of days the changes are undeniable. People are commenting on how healthy and happy she looks and a visit to her home office (which she had requested months earlier was magical accepted) the next morning.

Move 27 Things

To get the energy flowing in your home, start by focusing on what you want to manifest – your intention. Then begin moving things around. You can work on the whole house, a single room, a closet, or even a small drawer. The key is to have fun! Play music that lifts your spirit, dance, clap, ring a bell, or sing. When you see something you truly love, celebrate it and consider moving it to a more prominent place where you can enjoy it even more.

Have a piece of artwork or furniture that's been in the same spot for years? Try moving it to a fresh location.

If something no longer serves you, move it to a designated spot for gifting, donating, repurposing, or, if necessary, throwing away. While it can feel challenging to let things go, holding onto items that no longer serve you drains your energy. Release them and allow the space – and your energy – to open up. Let this be a reminder to only bring into your home what truly supports or inspires you.

So, Why 27 Things?

In feng shui, nine is considered a magic number. All multiples of nine reduce back to nine:

$$9 \times 2 = 18 \rightarrow 1 + 8 = 9$$
$$9 \times 3 = 27 \rightarrow 2 + 7 = 9$$
$$9 \times 4 = 36 \rightarrow 3 + 6 = 9$$

Moving 18, 27, or 36 items brings even more energy to your space and adds a layer of mindfulness (energy) to your manifestation. Keep your intention at the forefront as you move items – whether rearranging furniture, moving artwork, or clearing a small drawer.

Remember, the goal is to feel good and enjoy the process. You're creating a Magnetic Home – a space that makes you feel lighter, happier, and energized. If your energy isn't up for big changes, start small. Freeing up energy in your home frees up energy within you. Think of it like paying off credit cards: each card you pay off frees up financial resources and makes it easier to pay off the next credit card until finally, it's all clean and clear.

As you continue to infuse your home with your intention, placing the things you love where they feel right and keeping your space clear, your life will begin to align with your desires. Synchronicities will become a regular part of your experience.

Once you've moved your 27 (or 36) things,
pause and check in with yourself:

Now, describe your overall feeling in one or two sentences.

Next, rate how you feel about your home on a scale of 1 to 10:

$$1 - 2 - 3 - 4 - 5 - 6 - 7 - 8 - 9 - 10$$

The ultimate goal is always to feel better in your home – and in your life. Placing your intention on feeling good is one of the most important vibrational shifts you can make. Another repeatable Abraham Hicks philosophy for your mind and soul to remember and take to heart...

"It's important that you feel good."

~Abraham Hicks

Notes

Notes

Notes

Chapter 2

Feng Shui

The Secret Behind the Secret

Whether they realize it or not, the best manifestors use their home or office as a magnet for their dreams. Maybe it's as simple as creating a vision wall, arranging a sacred altar, or writing affirmations across the bathroom mirror. Whatever the form, the environment is speaking to the Universe – sending signals about what they're ready to receive.

Take Rhonda Byrne for example. She is the Australian author and producer best known for *The Secret* (2006). Rhonda had a big dream: she wanted *The Secret* to be a worldwide hit and to be interviewed on *The Oprah Winfrey Show*. But in the beginning, momentum was slow. Her vision felt stalled.

Enter Marie Diamond, one of the master teachers in *The Secret* and an internationally recognized feng shui expert. When Marie visited Rhonda's home, she identified areas where the energy was literally blocking her success. Rhonda's home was unintentionally sending mixed signals to the Universe. Marie suggested specific feng shui adjustments – moving her desk into the command position, enhancing her Fame and Reputation area, and placing a globe and a copy of *O Magazine* in her Partnership corner. Within months, *The Secret* was not only published as a book, but Rhonda was also invited to sit on

Oprah's stage. That's the magnetic power of aligning your home with your vision.

Feng shui is what I like to call the OG (original gangster) of manifesting. Long before we heard of the Law of Attraction, people were practicing geomancy – reading the energy of the land, water, wind, and stars to place homes, temples, and gardens in cosmic alignment. This practice goes back thousands of years. The words "feng shui" literally translate to wind (feng) and water (shui) – the two natural elements most responsible for carrying energy and its flow.

Think of it this way: too much wind becomes a storm; too little, and the air feels stifled. Too much water floods and destroys; too little becomes stagnant and lifeless. Feng shui is about finding the flow, the balance, the sweet spot where energy moves with vitality through your life and home.

You don't need to be Chinese, Buddhist, or part of any tradition to benefit from this practice. Feng shui transcends religion – it's about energy, intention, and harmony. You can call on Jesus, God, Allah, Mother Mary, The Sparkles, Pachamama, Archangel Michael, or any source you choose. What matters most is your intention and the awareness you bring to your space.

As I've traveled the world, I've seen how every culture has its own rituals for blessing a home. In Greece, people use the evil eye to ward off harm. In Peru, when a new home is built, the community presents the family with two bulls and a cross to place on the rooftop for protection and good fortune. Across the globe, humans instinctively design spaces not just for comfort, but to invite in prosperity and harmony.

This is the essence of creating your *Magnetic Home*. There is no "perfect" or "wrong" way. Favor your personal style. Place objects where they light up your heart. Use your intuition, invent rituals, and most importantly, make changes when you are in a good mood and in a high vibration. Energy carries through your actions. A few mindful adjustments go a long way.

So, trust your instincts, have fun with the process, and remember – you're not just decorating your home. You're tuning it like a sacred instrument, aligning it with the frequency of the life you desire.

The Fundamental Principles of Manifesting Feng Shui

Manifesting Feng Shui isn't about moving your couch to the "perfect" angle or obsessing over which direction your front door faces – it's about learning to play with energy. Imagine your home as a living, breathing vision board, constantly broadcasting your intentions (or lack of them) out to the Universe. The fundamentals of Manifesting Feng Shui give you the keys to tune into the channel you want to broadcast. With a few simple tweaks – and a whole lot of fun – you can align your space with your highest frequency, making your home not just a place to live, but a magnet for the life you're ready to create.

Everything is Energy

The Universe, and everything in it, is energy. You probably learned in grade school that matter is made of atoms, and atoms are made of protons, neutrons, and electrons. But here's the fascinating part: atoms are mostly space.

If an atom were the size of a football stadium, the nucleus would be no bigger than a marble in the center, while the electrons would be moving through an enormous field of possibility around it. What we experience as "solid" matter is energy in constant motion – always vibrating, always alive.

When you understand this, you begin to see your home, your belongings, and even your own body not as fixed objects, but as energy fields dancing in relationship with one another.

Intention is Most Important

Our thoughts are energy, too. When we place intention behind them, we direct the quantum field to manifest what we desire – we can magnify this by increasing the vibration of those things closest to us, like our homes.

Think of two tuning forks. Strike one, and the other begins to hum in resonance. Or picture a row of metronomes that, when set in motion, eventually sync up with one another. Energy seeks harmony.

The same principle is at work in your life. Your home is always syncing with your vibration. This is why every action – decluttering a drawer, moving a sofa, sweeping the floor, even taking a nap – becomes infinitely more powerful when done with intention. Energy responds to clarity.

Your Space Reflects Your Life

Our homes reflect our inner world. A cluttered room often mirrors a feeling of overwhelm. A light-filled, orderly space reflects inner calm. And beyond what you can see and feel, traditional feng shui gives us a powerful map to overlay on our floor plans. This energetic blueprint reveals how different areas of your home correspond to areas of your life – wealth, health, relationships, etc. When we align these spaces, we're not just rearranging furniture – we're rearranging our lives. Your home becomes not just where you live, but a mirror of who you are and a tool for who you are becoming.

The Spirit of All Things

Our homes and belongings carry energy, memory, and spirit. They hold the stories of our lives. If you slow down and listen, your home will speak to you. Sometimes it's a whisper – *move this chair, release this object*. Other times it's a deep knowing – *a change must be made for me to grow with you*. When you honor this spirit, you enter into a sacred partnership with your space. Together, you create flow, harmony, and magnetism.

Life Is Meant to Be a Game

We are here to play, to create, to experience the miracle of life fully. Too often, we sit in the stands, critiquing how others are playing, or worse – we stay home, safe in our recliners, analyzing the game but never stepping onto the field ourselves.

Manifesting Feng Shui invites you back onto the field. Not because it guarantees winning, but because life is meant to be lived in motion, in alignment, in joyful participation. It's not about winning or losing. It's about playing with your whole heart, giving it everything you have, and trusting that the Universe will meet you where your energy is.

When you live this way, your home transforms into a magnetic vortex – an energetic match to your deepest desires – and your life begins to unfold in miraculous ways.

One of my favorite quotes is from Jim Rohn, the philosopher:

"Setting a big goal is not about achieving the goal. It's about becoming the person it takes to achieve the goal."

~Jim Rohn

People are going to judge you no matter what. That's what people do. They'll have opinions, offer advice you didn't ask for, and sometimes project their own fears onto your dreams. The secret? Keep what you are doing to yourself and stay focused on what you want. Have fun with it. Trust your own vibe more than their voices. Before long, the very same people who doubted you will be leaning in, curious, and asking, *"How are you pulling all this magic off?"*

Chapter 3

The Magnetic Game Board

Did you love board games as a kid? Maybe you couldn't get enough of them – or maybe they weren't your thing. Personally, I've always loved games. *"PASS GO, Collect $200!"* is burned into my memory from countless Monopoly marathons on snowy South Dakota days when it was too cold to play outside.

That's why I like to call this feng shui bagua the Magnetic Game Board. If you enjoy board games, you'll love this – because it's like playing with the energy of your space by moving things around to create more flow, abundance, health and joy in your life.

Traditionally, this map was an octagon (Ba-Gua literally means "eight sides" in Chinese,) with each section representing one of the eight directions: north, northeast, east, southeast, south, southwest, west, and northwest. At the very center is Health – because let's face it, if you don't have your health, you don't have much of anything.

In the early 1970s, Professor Thomas Lin Yun – later honored as His Holiness Grandmaster Lin Yun – brought feng shui to the United States and gave it a modern twist. Traditional schools like The Compass School relied on a luopan (a special compass) to chart energy through directions, landforms, and time cycles. Lin Yun, however, simplified the practice for Western students and introduced what became known as Black

Sect Tantric Buddhist Feng Shui (BTB). Simplifying feng shui made it more accessible to all of us.

Here's the game-changing part: he reshaped the bagua into a rectangle divided into nine equal sections, like a tic-tac-toe board, with Health still in the center. Instead of orienting it with a compass, the map is aligned with the front door – the home's main entrance – making it simple and practical for anyone to use for more affect.

Even more importantly, Lin Yun emphasized that *intention* was even more powerful than physical placement. He brought equal focus to the invisible: intuition, spiritual practice, and personal cultivation. He even encouraged the use of modern healing tools like affirmations, crystals, mirrors, aromatherapy, and art.

Some traditionalists criticized BTB as being "too simplified," but thousands of people around the world embraced it for one reason: it works. It helps people shift energy quickly and intentionally – in their homes, their relationships, and their lives.

Now you can begin to see how your own home becomes a living gameboard for manifesting what you would like to have and experience.

The Nine Life Areas of the Magnetic Game Board

PROSPERITY	FAME & REPUTATION	PARTNERSHIP
FAMILY OF ORIGIN	HEALTH	CHILDREN/ CREATIVITY
SELF-KNOWLEDGE/ WISDOM	CAREER	HELPFUL PEOPLE & TRAVEL

↑ ALIGN TO FRONT DOOR WALL ↑

Prosperity

This area governs abundance in all its forms – not only money, but also blessings, opportunities, and a sense of richness in life. It represents royalty. When balanced, it radiates gratitude, generosity, and the ability to receive.

Fame & Reputation

This is how you are seen in the world – your visibility, being respected, your integrity, and the legacy you leave behind. It relates to recognition, confidence, and shining authentically in your Divine Light so your gifts are seen.

Partnership

This area reflects love, romance, marriage and deep connections. It embodies harmony, communication, and mutual support in relationships, whether the relationships are romantic ones, business, or friendships.

Family of Origin

Here we honor our roots, ancestry, and the support systems that ground us. It's about loyalty, unity, and drawing strength from our heritage and those who came before us. It is also about new beginnings, fresh starts.

Health

The heart of the Magnetic Game Board, this area influences vitality, balance, and overall well-being. It represents harmony between body, mind, and spirit – the hub from which all other life areas flow. It is the most important area of the Bagua.

Children & Creativity

This area governs joy, playfulness, imagination, and authenticity. It reflects the children and grandchildren of the home. Also, the projects, ideas, and creations we bring into the world.

Knowledge & Wisdom

This is the area of learning, inner growth, spiritual insight, and clarity. It represents meditation, study, and the wisdom we gain through reflection and experience.

Career

This area relates to your journey through life – your calling, work, and the flow of opportunities. It's about living your soul's purpose and moving with the current of life, rather than against it.

Helpful People/Travel

This area governs mentors, guides, and supportive relationships, as well as journeys of all kinds. It's the energy of divine assistance – the right people showing up at the right time, and the adventure of exploring new horizons. This is the area of synchronicities.

A STORY

Love at First Sight. My Discovery of Feng Shui.

I was completely gobsmacked the first time I picked up a feng shui book. As I flipped through the pages, I kept whispering to myself, "I know this." I would turn another page, read a section and again think, "I know this." It felt like coming home to a place I had always known yet had never visited.

That day, I had been magnetically drawn to the feng shui section and I left Barnes & Noble with thirteen books cradled in a heavy white plastic bag, my heart bursting with curiosity and wonder. I was eight months pregnant with my first child, yet those uncomfortable, often sleepless nights were spent devouring every word, soaking up knowledge like a sponge. One morning, as I lay in bed reading yet another book, my husband looked over and commented on my voracious appetite for feng shui. I told him, simply, "I'm going to be a feng shui master."

He looked at me like I was a foolish child. "That's impossible. It takes thirty years."

I smiled inside. Well, if it takes thirty years, it takes thirty years. I will be a feng shui master. At 32, for the first time, I knew of something I wanted beyond being a wife and a mom. This was the beginning of my rapid ascent into spirituality.

I believe my daughter – my guru even before she was born – led me to those books, opening a magical portal to something greater than I had ever imagined. Or maybe it was destiny. Or Heaven Luck. Whatever you call it, it was perfect timing.

Just months earlier, I had begun to wonder if I could ever have children. After facing precancerous growths and seeing my mom's early hysterectomy, doubts started to creep in. Yet, I had always dreamed of being a mom, never thinking of a career outside my family and ranch life. And then, the universe winked.

At a fundraiser for micro-lending to women in third-world countries, my eyes fell on a 4-foot by 4-foot Jiang Tie Fang serigraph titled *Mother and Child*. The child sat contentedly in the mother's lap as she curled protectively around, radiating pure love and tenderness. In that moment, something inside me cracked open – I was instantly overwhelmed, tears streaming as I felt the depth of that embrace I saw before me. I had to have it. Call it impulse, call it destiny – call it b'shert – but in my heart, I knew it was meant to be to have that beautiful piece of artwork in my home.

I bought it, and the large print with a generous frame wouldn't fit in my car, and when friends delivered it to me, I discovered it barely fit in my small home. There was only one spot large enough – my Children/Creativity wall in the dining room. I hung it, oblivious to feng shui, manifesting, or energy. And yet... eighteen months later, I was married, pregnant, and living the life I had longed for at that time.

Emotion → Action → Placement → Magic

That was all it took. One heartfelt yearning, acted upon, became a reality. And then two more children followed; three under the age of four in the blink of an eye.

From that moment at Barnes and Noble, I was hooked. I learned the intricacies of the Nine Life Areas and used this "gameboard" to intentionally enhance my life. Energy, intention, and small adjustments – clearing clutter, enhancing the front door, honoring bathrooms – created palpable shifts. Friends noticed the change without me saying a word! They felt it. I started consulting and making suggestions in their homes at their request.

Soon, I knew I wanted to study with a feng shui master to deepen my practice. Carole Hyder of the Wind and Water School of Feng Shui became my guide, showing me hands-on how to conduct effective consultations and how to connect energy with intention. I poured myself into teaching feng shui, sharing this wisdom with hundreds of students and clients, helping them create magnetic homes and lives filled with possibility.

Feng shui wasn't just a tool – it was the key that unlocked my life, revealing the power of intention, destiny, and the magic that unfolds when we listen to our hearts.

Creating Your Magnetic Game Board

There's treasure in them there hills! Think of this step like unfolding your very own treasure map – you're stretching the Magnetic Game Board across your home floorplan to see where each of your Nine Life Areas "live." Picture it like a scene straight out of *The da Vinci Code*: you, pencil in hand, leaning over your floorplan like Nicholas Cage lining up clues, tracing secret codes and symbols that reveal hidden treasure. Only instead of ancient mysteries, you're decoding the energy of your home. When the Magnetic Game Board lines up just right, suddenly your space isn't just walls and furniture, it's a mirror of your soul's journey, showing you where energy flows freely, where it gets stuck, and where the hidden treasures are waiting for you to claim them.

Now, before you start imagining graph paper nightmares or complicated blueprints, take a deep breath. This is not architecture class; it's energy play. The goal is not perfection; it's clarity. You're simply creating a "snapshot" of how energy flows through your space right now.

Most homes aren't perfect squares or rectangles. Some have wings, garages, porches, or quirky corners that stick out or sink in. That's all part of the story. Every bump, nook, or curve has meaning – and often reveals hidden treasures or opportunities for adjustment.

Here's what you'll need: a floorplan of your home (from the builder, realtor, or sketched by you,) a ruler, a pencil, and possibly a long tape measure if you want to get precise. Once you've got your plan in front of you, you'll learn how to line up the Magnetic Game Board with your front door and lay the gameboard over your entire home.

This is where the magic begins – where lines on paper reveal how your space is shaping your life.

Step 1: Print or Draw Your Floor Plan

- ✓ If you have architectural drawings, great! If not, you can use a tape measure and graph paper (or an online design tool) and begin to map out your home.
- ✓ Make sure your drawing includes all walls, doors, and major openings. And include where bathroom fixtures, stairways and stove are located.
- ✓ Keep it to scale so proportions are accurate.
- ✓ TIP: Once you have your floorplan, scan it or make a couple extra copies – it's easy to make little mistakes, and this way you can play around laying out the Magnetic Game Board without worry.

Step 2: Draw the Magnetic Game Board on Your Floorplan

Grab a ruler and pencil with the intention of drawing a large rectangle or square around the footprint of the house, including an attached garage or screened-in porch.

If your home isn't a perfect rectangle (most are not) you may see some areas of your home sticking out of the rectangle and some areas of the rectangle missing pieces of your home. These are referred to as *extensions* and *missing pieces*.

Use this assessment to determine where you would draw the outside line for the Magnetic Game Board:

✓ If one side of the house is irregular, measure the full length of that one side of the house, assess where more than half of the full length of the house would be. Place the outside line of the Magnetic Game Board along the longest measurement that includes more than half the total length. See below.

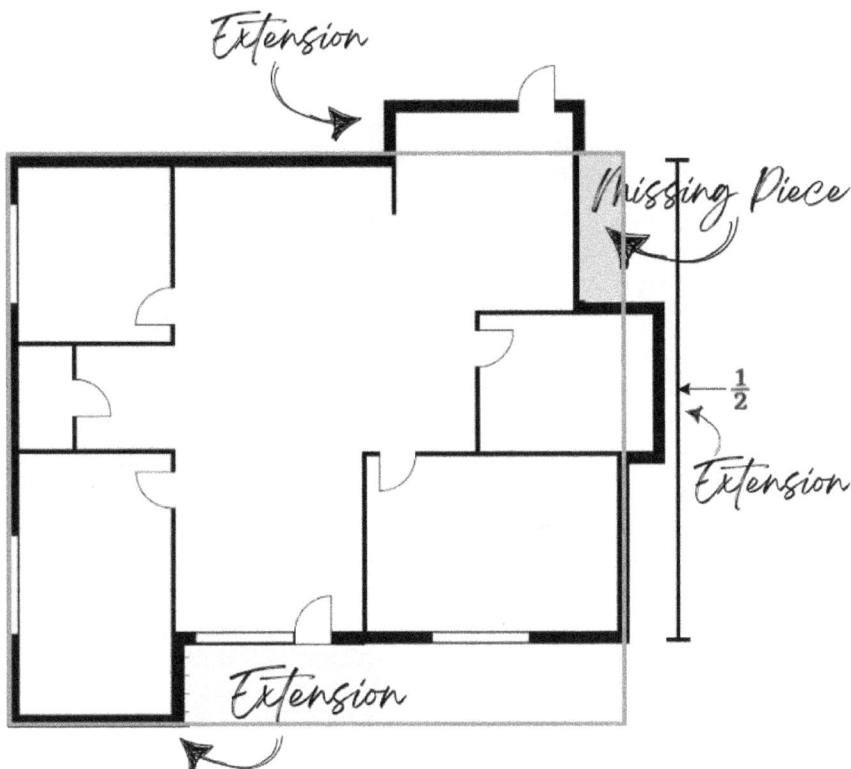

Sometimes, you will have a missing piece in the middle of the Magnetic Game Board. If the length of two outside pieces added together equals more than half the length of the house, then you use the outside measurements.

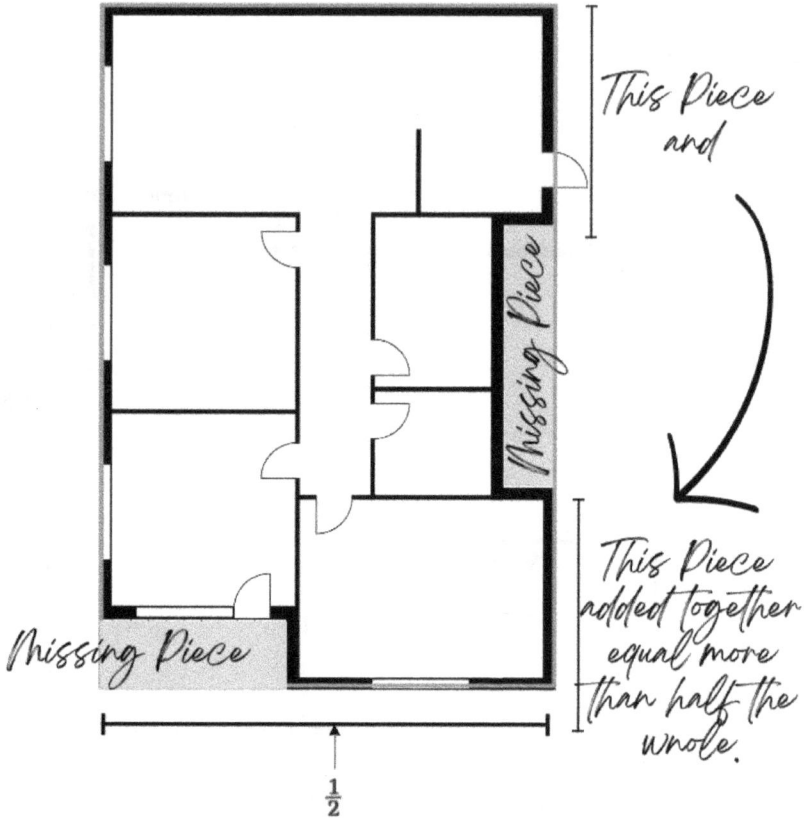

This Piece and

Missing Piece

Missing Piece

This Piece added together equal more than half the whole.

$\frac{1}{2}$

THERE IS ONE EXCEPTION TO THIS RULE!

✓ **The front door cannot be in an extension**, you will draw the outside of the Magnetic Game Board to include the front door, even if it's only a small, enclosed portico on the front of the home and leaves one or two large missing pieces. See next page.

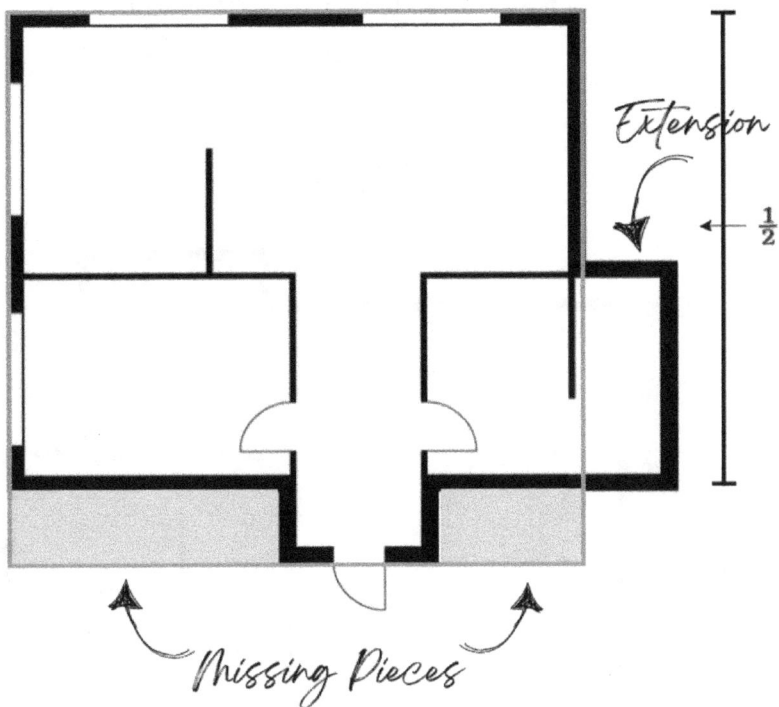

Extension

$\frac{1}{2}$

Missing Pieces

note

If your home is L-shaped or U-shaped, I recommend drawing the outside of the Magnetic Game Board such that all pieces are inside the Magnetic Game Board.

Step 3: Divide the Magnetic Game Board into a 3 × 3 grid (like a tic-tac-toe board) with all areas being equal sizes.

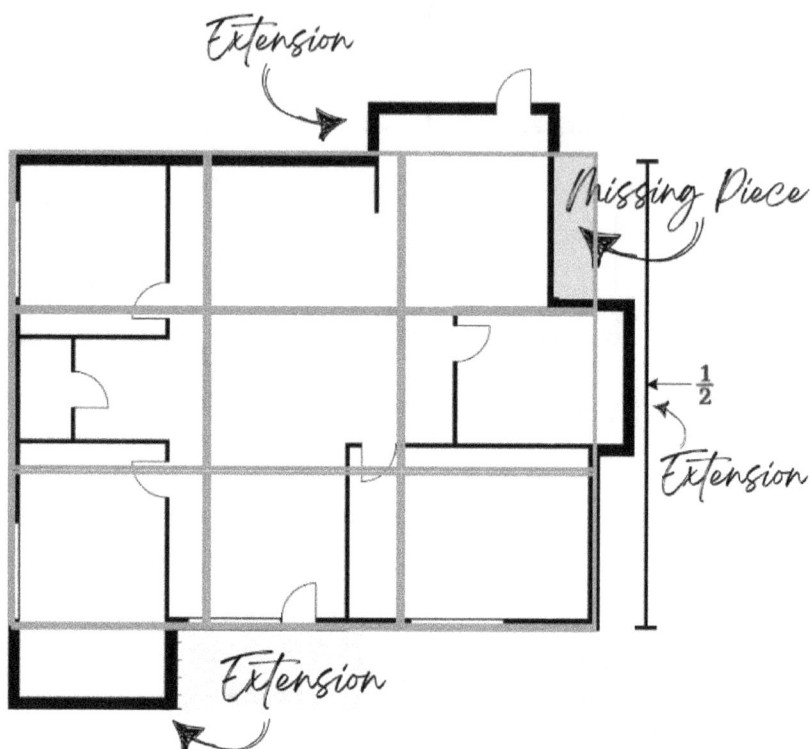

Extension

Missing Piece

$\frac{1}{2}$

Extension

Extension

Align the bottom row of the Magnetic Game Board (Knowledge & Wisdom / Career/ Helpful People & Travel) with the wall containing your main front door.

If you were to stand at your front door looking in, the back left corner is Prosperity, the back middle is Fame & Reputation, and the back right corner is Partnership. See below.

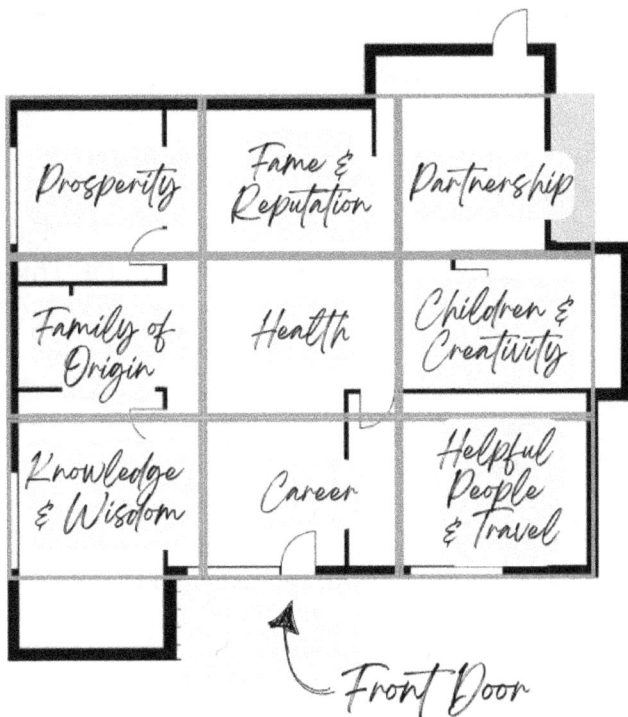

In this example, you can see extensions in Knowledge & Wisdom, Children & Creativity, Fame & Reputation and Partnership. There is a missing piece in Partnership.

Celebrate and Do Your Happy Dance!

When you get your Magnetic Game Board laid out over your floor plan be sure and give yourself a big pat on the back and Celebrate Your Success! Get up and do a little happy dance around the house or have that ice cream! You deserve it! This is the hardest part for most of us.

Common Questions about the Magnetic Game Board (and Easy Answers!)

- **Do I include the garage?** Yes, if it's attached. If it's detached, no.
- **What if part of my house sticks out in front (like a garage)?**
    - If the "jut out" is more than half the length of that side, draw your rectangle around it. This creates a *missing piece*.
    - If the jut out is less than half, draw your rectangle along the longest wall. This creates an *extension*.
    - **Exception:** The front door. The Magnetic Game Board must always align with your front door wall, never placed inside an extension.
- **Is a missing piece bad?** Not at all. It just means that Life Area isn't naturally supported so that will be one of the first things we will adjust for first. There are simple feng shui cures to bring this energy in and I tell you, the results can be Ah-mazing!
- **Is a porch included?** If it's fully enclosed, Yes. Even if it is screened in as long as there is a floor, roof and 4 walls. If it's open, no.
- **What about a split-level home?** Use the top floor – it holds the strongest energy.
- **Do I have to use a floor plan?** No. If you live in a smaller, less complicated home or you are using feng shui in a room, or another level of the house, you can measure the area, divide it into thirds and mark the corners of the Life Areas with painter's tape to identify the Nine Life Areas. You can leave the tape for a few days so you get a feel for what is happening in each Life Area.

- **What if I have two or more levels?** The main floor holds the strongest energy so it gets the greatest attention. For making adjustments, you can lay out the Magnetic Game Board over the basement or upstairs based on where you enter that level, not the front door of the home.

Chapter 4

Revealing Your Authentic Self

Before we do too much heavy lifting like moving furniture or picking paint colors, the first and most powerful step is connecting with your authentic self. Your authentic self is your *light self* – your highest vibration of being. When you live in alignment with this essence, your energy naturally resonates at a higher frequency, and your home can become a true reflection of that brilliance.

In this chapter, you'll uncover:

- ✓ **Your Core Values** – the foundation of who you are. These rarely change and are the compass that guides your choices.
- ✓ **Your Design Style** – what feels like *you* in a space, from textures and colors to simplicity or abundance.
- ✓ **Your Lifestyle Lens** – do you thrive on experiences or possessions, adventure or serenity?

Taking time to understand these layers of yourself is like finding hidden treasures. When you live by your values and design your space to reflect them, you unlock one of the most powerful forms of energy alignment. Because when your home reflects your truth... that's pure magic.

Identifying Your Core Values

Instructions:

✓ Read through the list of values.
✓ Check the ones that resonate most with you.
✓ Then, circle, highlight or put stars next to the ones that are most important to you until you have your Top 5 Core Values.

☐ Spirituality
☐ Intuition
☐ Creativity
☐ Learning / Knowledge
☐ Growth / Expansion
☐ Adventure
☐ Freedom
☐ Freedom to Choose
☐ Free Spirit
☐ Tradition
☐ Authenticity
☐ Honesty
☐ Integrity
☐ Dancing
☐ Excellence
☐ Trust
☐ Lack of Pretense
☐ Self-Expression
☐ Full Self-Expression
☐ Solid Family Relationships
☐ Friendship
☐ Romance
☐ Compassion
☐ Kindness
☐ Being Active

☐ Community
☐ Collaboration
☐ Partnership
☐ Comradeship
☐ Nurturing
☐ Connectedness
☐ To Be Known
☐ Humor
☐ Lightness
☐ Service
☐ Contribution
☐ Parties with Friends
☐ Leadership
☐ Encouragement
☐ Making a Difference
☐ Participation
☐ Nature
☐ Acknowledgment
☐ Religion
☐ Functionality
☐ Safety
☐ Emotional Intelligence
☐ Forward the Action
☐ Risk Taking
☐ Health
☐ Name Brands

- ☐ Vitality
- ☐ Balance
- ☐ Simplicity
- ☐ Peace/Serenity
- ☐ Joy
- ☐ Harmony
- ☐ Craziness
- ☐ Beauty
- ☐ Orderliness
- ☐ Elegance
- ☐ Success
- ☐ Accomplishment
- ☐ Vibrant
- ☐ Colorful
- ☐ Recognition
- ☐ High Performance
- ☐ Prosperity
- ☐ Creativity
- ☐ Innovation

- ☐ Focus
- ☐ Time with Family
- ☐ Design
- ☐ Accuracy
- ☐ Entrepreneurialism
- ☐ Empowerment
- ☐ Personal Power
- ☐ Independence
- ☐ Efficiency
- ☐ Spiritual Pursuits
- ☐ Financial Security
- ☐ Going to the Gym
- ☐ Watching TV
- ☐ Being a Partner
- ☐ Being a Parent
- ☐ Dependable
- ☐ Independence
- ☐ Personal Development
- ☐ Flying Solo

My Top 5 Core Values:

1. _____
2. _____
3. _____
4. _____
5. _____

Discovering Your Design Style

Your home should feel like *you* – not a showroom, not a magazine spread, but a reflection of your authentic self. I call this, *Styled by Inspiration*. This little checklist will help you uncover your natural style and design preferences so you can make choices that truly light you up.

Atmosphere and Mood

Do you feel most comfortable in spaces that are:

☐ Cozy and warm

☐ Bright and airy

☐ Minimal and serene

☐ Vibrant and energizing

Color Palette

Which color families make you feel most alive

☐ Neutrals (whites, grays, taupes)

☐ Earth tones (browns, greens, terracotta)

☐ Pastels (soft pinks, blues, lavenders)

☐ Jewel tones (emerald, sapphire, ruby)

☐ Bold and bright (yellow, red, turquoise)

Shape and Form

Do you prefer:

☐ Clean, straight lines

☐ Rounded, organic shapes

☐ A mix of both

Texture and Materials

What do you naturally gravitate toward?

☐ Natural woods and stone

☐ Smooth, glossy finishes

☐ Soft, touchable fabrics (plush, velvet, wool)

☐ Sleek, modern metals or glass

Décor and Details

Which feels more "you"?

☐ Minimalist – just the essentials

☐ Eclectic – lots of personality and unique finds

☐ Classic – timeless and structured

☐ Spiritual – symbols, altars, meaningful art

Lighting

The light I love most is:

☐ Soft, warm glow (lamps, candles)

☐ Bright and clear (sunlight, overhead)

☐ Playful and creative (string lights, lanterns)

☐ A balance, depending on the mood

Connection to Nature

Which natural element makes you feel most supported?

☐ Plants and greenery

☐ Water features (fountains, aquariums, views of water)

☐ Stones and crystals
☐ Sunlight and fresh air

Personal Style Reflection

If your *personal fashion* style were a room, it would be:

☐ Chic and polished
☐ Cozy and comfortable
☐ Colorful and bold
☐ Simple and minimal
☐ Unique and expressive

reflect

What patterns do you notice in your answers? Does your current home reflect these preferences – or is there a disconnect between what you have and what you like?

Which 2-3 preferences feel *non-negotiable* for you moving forward?

MAGNETIC HOME

Looking Through Your Lifestyle Lens

This is less about what colors you like and how you want to live life within your four walls. The way you move through your day, the people you invite in, and how you use your space are all a part of what makes your Magnetic Home truly work for *you*. This quick checklist helps you see where your home can better support your daily flow and future dreams.

Daily Flow

When I walk through my home, I want to feel:

☐ Energized and ready for action

☐ Calm and peaceful

☐ Grounded and supported

☐ Inspired and creative

Social Vibe

My home is mostly for:

☐ Entertaining family and friends

☐ Quiet retreat and solitude

☐ A mix of both – sometimes lively, sometimes private

Work and Creativity

My home needs to support me most with:

☐ Focus and productivity (home office, study)

☐ Creativity and inspiration (art, writing, projects)

☐ Relaxation and restoration

☐ A little bit of everything

Health and Well-Being

What feels most important right now?

☐ Space for movement (yoga, exercise, stretching)

☐ Nourishment (a kitchen that inspires healthy meals)

☐ Deep rest (a cozy, restorative bedroom)

☐ Stress relief (meditation, baths, nature connection)

Travel and Mobility

How does your lifestyle flow?

☐ I'm home-centered and love my sanctuary

☐ I'm often on the go but want home to recharge me

☐ I travel a lot and need my home to feel simple and low-maintenance

Growth and Expansion

Right now, my home most needs to support:

☐ Career/business success

☐ Deeper relationships and connection

☐ Personal healing and self-care

☐ Spiritual practice and alignment

reflect

Where does your home currently *fit* your lifestyle – and where does it fall short? If your home were your teammate, how could it better support you in living your best life?

The Nine Life Areas Wheel

Take out a pen or a set of colored markers. Look at the wheel below, which is divided into the Nine Life Areas of the Magnetic Game Board. Reflect on how you feel you are doing in each of the Life Areas. If you feel strong and fulfilled in a particular area, fill in the entire section of the wheel. If you feel there is room for growth, shade in the section only to the level that represents your current sense of satisfaction.

This simple exercise gives you a clear visual snapshot of where your energy is balanced and where you may want to create more focus and alignment.

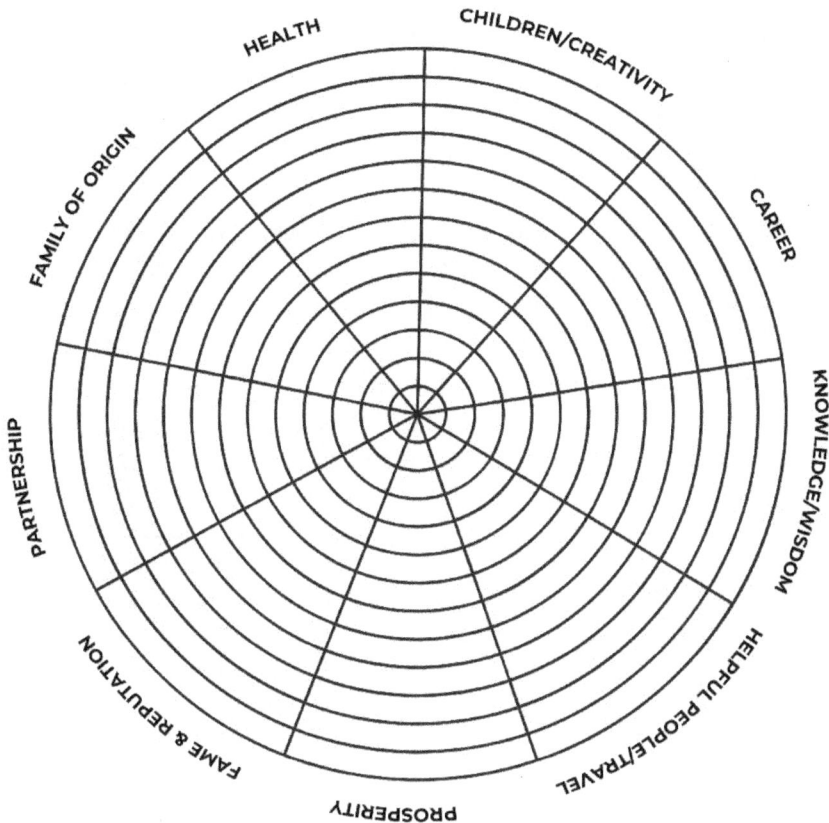

What is Your Wheel Telling You?

Take a look at your wheel. Is it smooth and balanced in the mid- to high-range, or does it feel more like a rollercoaster with highs in some areas and big dips in others? Imagine your Nine Life Areas Wheel as the tires on a car. Are you cruising down the highway with ease – or bumping along like an old jalopy with square wheels? Is there anything else that you notice?

Now, bring your Top Five Core Values, Design Style and Lifestyle back into focus. Compare them to the Nine Life Areas. Where are you in harmony, living with ease? And where do you feel the rub – those misalignments that quietly drain your energy?

This is your opportunity to spot the gaps, to name the areas that need a little more love, and to begin sealing up any energy leaks. Think of your Magnetic Game Board as the playground where you can align your home with your deepest values and your boldest dreams.

Ask yourself:

- ✓ Which areas feel most aligned with my values, design style and lifestyle and which feel most out of step?
- ✓ What specific improvements would light me up here?
- ✓ How might adjusting these areas in my home create a powerful shift in the life I'm calling in?

Choose Three Life Areas you want to focus on first:

Life Area #1: _____

Life Area #2: _____

Life Area #3: _____

Intention is Most Important

Your intention is the foundation of everything you create. What you focus on expands, so clarity is key. By setting a powerful, well-defined intention, you align your energy with what you want to manifest.

Clarify Your Intention

1. **Focus on What You Want**
   - Direct your attention toward what you desire, not what you want to avoid. The universe responds to your energy, keep your focus on what you want, not what you fear.

2. **Write It Down**
   - Use one or two sentences that clearly state your intention.
   - Write your intention several times a day for at least nine consecutive days.
   - If possible, use blue-lined white paper to support clarity and focus.

3. **Visualize in Action**
   - Train yourself to focus on what you want, especially the first ten or fifteen minutes when you first wake up. This is powerful manifesting time.
   - You can write your intention in the shower with a dry-erase marker. I have discovered that the shower is an excellent manifesting vortex. We "take" a shower. For many, it is the rare moment of the day when we are in the receiving flow vs. feeling like we are always doing or giving.
   - Create a dream board and put it where you see it often like near your bathroom mirror, at the foot of your bed or at your desk.

- Write about your intention daily using sensory words describing how you feel, what you see, the aromas, etc.

4. **Let Go of Attachment**
   - Release the "how" and "when."
   - Stay clear on what you want and review your intentions regularly.
   - Trust that the universe will deliver it to you in your perfect timing. The universe is always working in your favor.

5. **State Your Intentions Positively**
   - Avoid phrasing that focuses on lack or fear.
   - Instead of: "My intention is to not go into foreclosure," say: "My intention is to have a positive monthly cash flow of $2,000 or more by September 19, 20XX."

6. **Examples of Powerful Intentions**
   - "My intention is to receive an A in my social studies course."
   - "My intention is to have more than enough time, money, and resources to do what I want, when I want."
   - "My intention is to experience ease and grace in my life."

By consistently clarifying, writing, and feeling your intentions, you train your mind, your Reticular Activating System (RAS), and your energy to recognize opportunities that align with your desires. The clearer your intention, the easier it is for the universe to respond.

What are your intentions for your Top Three Life Areas?

On page 47 you chose your most important three life areas. Write your intentions for each area. Phrase your intention as though they are already happening, not something you're chasing or hoping for. The more specific you are, the more magnetic your results will be.

Intention #1: _____

Intention #2: _____

Intention #3: _____

reflect _____

Pause here and take a breath – you've just laid the foundation for attracting what you want. Simply getting clear on what you want begins to shift the energy around you, even before you move a single thing in your home. Close your eyes for a moment and breathe in these intentions. Imagine them sparkling like stardust, rising up and out as a siren's call to the Universe.

Chapter 5

Essential Adjustments

Take a moment to review your Magnetic Game Borad. Which life areas in your home have extensions (blessings) and which have missing pieces (gaps or challenges)? Extensions often feel like natural gifts, while missing areas may reveal where energy needs extra care.

Now, tune in. Does anything about your home feel "off" – or does it suddenly make perfect sense? Pay special attention to bathrooms and stairs, since these can act as drains on energy. Notice how what you see on your Magnetic Game Board might mirror the patterns playing out in your own life. Maybe your career is in the toilet (literally and figuratively.) Approach this with curiosity – journal, doodle, reflect. Let it feel playful and light.

Some adjustments are a priority so let's start with those.

- ✓ Locate the center of your home. This is the heartbeat of you and your home.
- ✓ Make adjustments for missing pieces. This is all about wholeness and completeness. You don't want to be missing any energy.
- ✓ Observe where you have bathrooms and stairs.

Find the Center (Your Center)

The center of your home is the center of you. When you are aligned, everything flows with greater ease – and the same is true for your home.

In the Indian tradition of Vastu, this sacred center is called the *Brahmasthan* – the place of creation. The teaching is simple: keep it open, light, and free. No clutter. No heavy furniture. And definitely no drains like bathrooms, kitchens, or staircases. This is your home's soul space, and like you, it needs to breathe.

In feng shui, the message echoes: the center represents Health, the life area that touches every other zone. When your health is vibrant, everything else gets easier. Support this area by keeping it clear, bright, and welcoming.

Here's how to find your home's center:

- On your Magnetic Game Board, draw a line from Prosperity to Helpful People/Travel.
- Draw another from Partnerships to Knowledge & Wisdom & Wisdom.
- Where the two lines meet is the heart of your home.

The Center

Go and actually stand in the center of your home. Close your eyes and notice: how does it feel? Is it open, grounded and alive - or does it feel cluttered, heavy and stagnant? If you feel called to move something, please do! Trust that nudge - your home is speaking to you.

I love creating sacred rituals because they shift energy so quickly. They don't have to be elaborate productions (though they can be if you enjoy that kind of sacred theater). Sometimes the smallest action – a candle, a flower, a quick tidy – creates the biggest change.

When it feels aligned, here's a simple and powerful way to begin infusing your Magnetic Home with fresh, supportive energy. Feel free to do as much or as little as feels right.

Ritual for Honoring The Center

Calling Your Energy Back to You and Releasing Any Energy that Doesn't Belong to You

This isn't just a ritual – it's a reset. By centering your home, you are centering yourself. You are calling your energy back, strengthening your foundation, and anchoring in balance.

> ✓ **Prepare:** Freshen up with a shower. Wear your favorite color (yellow is beautiful here – it activates

the Health area). Light candles, incense, or bring flowers.

✓ **Clear the space:** Remove clutter or heavy objects. Even a few minutes of tidying creates an instant shift. Put some of your favorite essential oils on a cloth and wipe the area clean.

✓ **Call your energy back to you:** Standing in the center, place your hand on your heart and ask out loud:

"Dear Mother/Father/God: Please return to me any of my energy that is being held by other people or past situations. Please return to the rightful owner any energy that I've been holding onto that doesn't belong to me. It is done."

Silently, invite your home to do the same – to release and return any energy that doesn't belong in the space and to bring in new energy to support your dreams and endeavors.

✓ **Seal the center:** Place a small red dot on the floor or wall with intention or hang a round-faceted crystal from the ceiling with a red string (cut in a multiple of nine). Imagine it as a radiant disco ball, scattering sparkling light that dances joyfully into every corner of your home while keeping you centered and grounded.

✓ **Pause in stillness:** Stand or sit quietly, hand over your heart, and feel your energy – and your home's energy – fully restored, clear, and centered.

The Beauty of a Missing Piece

You might be surprised to hear me say this, but a missing piece in your home isn't a bad thing. In fact, I see it as a little wink from the universe – a reminder that life is always guiding you. A missing piece often highlights your **Heaven Luck** – those blessings, opportunities, or support that come from beyond your control. With awareness, you can partner with this energy and bring fresh life into that space.

Once you *see* the missing piece, you've already shifted the energy. Awareness itself is powerful. From there, it's time for a little magic-making with some simple, playful adjustments:

- ✓ **Round Mirror on the Wall** – Place it where the missing piece would be, symbolically "pushing the wall out" and completing the space. Want to keep it subtle? You can even hide the mirror behind another picture. The energy is still there being held by your intention.

- ✓ **Pointed Crystal in the Ground** – Like acupuncture for your home. Ceremoniously tamp a pointed crystal down into the earth where the missing piece would extend, releasing blocked energy and calling fresh flow into that life area or areas. Use a clear crystal or a color that corresponds to the Life Area color.

- ✓ **Red Dot of Completion** – A simple red dot acts like a seal, pulling the space together. You can also use red thread or ribbon to draw the missing line energetically, even burying it discreetly in the ground to extend the home's footprint. Red is the highest-vibration color – it is used to cure energy. Red is auspicious in many cultures around the world and you can add it to every ceremony.
    - ○ One of my favorite tricks? A bottle of red fingernail polish purchased just for your Magnetic Home adjustments. It's fun, intentional, and powerful. You can add a master Reiki or sacred geometry symbol to the bottle for even more magnetic power. It's all about intention.

- ✓ **Living Energy** – You can add a garden in that space with the intention of completing the space. Or use your intuition and place a potted plant, plant a shrub, or hang a wind chime to symbolically carry energy into the

56

missing zone. Use the color associated with that Life Area.

These simple actions carry powerful meaning: nothing is truly missing – it is restored. These little adjustments are receivers for your home – subtle yet deeply effective. They tell the universe, *"Yes, I'm ready for energy to flow here."* Remember, the beauty of a missing piece is that it gives you a chance to play. It highlights where you're ready to grow, and with a few mindful touches, you can invite fresh opportunities, blessings, and vitality into that part of your life.

A STORY

The Missing Piece

I was called to the home of a couple with a big dream: building a $500 million power plant. Their home was impressive – grand enough to make you notice – and it was clear they ran a few successful businesses from there. I met the wife first: crisp white blouse, tailored slacks, and the unmistakable energy of a woman who managed her own lucrative business buying and selling office equipment.

The main topic? Her husband's project. For over a year, he had received an overwhelming amount of publicity regarding his project – radio, TV, newspapers – but no investors were biting. Not one penny. Something was off.

When I looked at their floor plan, the answer leapt out at me. Their Fame and Reputation area was on fire. There was an extension with not one, but two fireplaces. With Fame and Reputation being a fire element, no wonder the publicity was coming in hot!

But here's the twist: the problem wasn't visibility. Their Prosperity area was completely missing. Nada. Not even a sliver.

They had all the attention in the world, but the energy that captures financial flow simply wasn't there.

I gave her a simple, affordable adjustment and powerful affirmation to energetically complete the prosperity corner – a purple pointed, faceted crystal she tamped into the corner of the missing piece. Within a week, the universe answered. The wife called, practically bouncing off the walls. Her husband had just received $100 million in seed funding – the exact push needed to kick-start the project. She was confident the remaining $400 million would follow soon after.

A missing piece can be a blessing. Making one simple adjustment can be like tapping into a hidden vein of oil that's been blocked for years. Once the energy starts to flow, it gushes – and you can stand back and watch the magic happen.

Adjust for Any Other Missing Pieces

Look around your home. Is there a corner of a room that feels "off" or empty? That missing piece could be quietly holding back the energy you most want – money, opportunities, recognition, or even joy.

Awareness is everything. Once you see it, a small, intentional adjustment can unlock the flow. Place a crystal, hang a round mirror, add a splash of color, or use a symbolic object – anything that completes the space energetically. Just like the prosperity corner in that couple's home, sometimes all it takes is a mindful, simple shift in your mind or in your home to open the door for something ah-mazing to come to fruition.

Bathrooms: Is Your Energy Flushing Away?

Bathrooms are magical places – and a little tricky. Water can be a powerful energy for manifesting, especially the shower, but left unattended, water can also drain your energy. Think of it like this: energy spirals down a toilet, taking with it vital life area energy instead of sticking around to support you. The shower and sink are draining, too.

The good news? There are simple, fun adjustments you can do to save – or even reverse – that flow:

Toilets:

- ✓ **Round mirror above the bowl** – The intention is to flip the energy upward, reversing the downward vortex. (Full disclosure: I haven't personally tried this one, but it's a classic feng shui tweak!)
- ✓ **Seeds on the tank** – Rice, birdseed, sesame, or mustard seeds. Imagine the water spiraling up, germinating life, creating positive, growing energy feeding the life area you want supported.
- ✓ **Plants** – Real or beautiful faux plants on the back of the toilet, like seeds, the water comes up to nourish the plants.

Toilets, Sinks, Showers and Tubs

- ✓ **Neutralize the flow with red** – Use red electrician's tape, a magic marker, string or your magic red Magnetic Home fingernail polish around the drainpipe. Red seals the area, protecting and enhancing flow.
- ✓ **Building a new home or remodeling?** – It's really easy to use red paint and paint the drains after the plumber is there and before flooring and fixtures are installed.
- ✓ **Mindful closure** – Close drains when not in use and affirm your good fortune, abundance, and prosperity. Your intention carries as much or more energy as any physical adjustment.

With just a few playful tweaks, your bathroom can go from an energy drain to an energy boost. Water is powerful, and with awareness and intention, you can keep that vitality spiraling up, supporting your life instead of slipping away.

Stairs Got You Feeling Run Down?

Stairs are more than a way to get from one floor to another – they carry energy down. If you have stairs in your Health area, you could literally be feeling *run down*. Fatigue, low energy, and feeling drained? Your space might be reflecting your life.

I remember presenting to a group of women when one lady came up afterward. She said, "I don't believe in feng shui, but if I did... what would the stairs in the middle of my home represent?" I told her they represent feeling run down. Her jaw dropped. She said, "Oh my gosh. When we moved into our new home, I just felt so exhausted. I even thought we had a carbon monoxide leak!"

Then she timidly asked, "What's the adjustment for that?"

I laughed and said, "Hang a round-faceted crystal at the top of the stairs." Think of it like a disco ball for energy. It slows down the rush of energy, breaks it into little sparkles, and spreads it evenly so you have smooth, even flow instead of too much energy flowing in one direction.

Here are some other adjustments to keep energy moving smoothly on stairs:

- ✓ **Plants** – Place a small, healthy plant near landings or at the top of the stairs. It helps energize the area and brings vitality upward.
- ✓ **Mirrors** – Hang a small mirror on the wall beside the staircase to redirect energy and brighten the path.
- ✓ **Red thread along the railing or red dots at the top and bottom of the stairs** – This adds movement to the energy as you walk up and down, keeping chi lively and on point.
- ✓ **Mindful intention** – Every time you go up or down the stairs, take a deep breath and imagine energy flowing with you, instead of zipping past you.

Stairs going straight to the front door?

That can be problematic. It represents money flowing straight out the door. A couple of simple adjustments are:

- ✓ Place a money plant near the front door to attract and circulate abundance.
- ✓ Use a small basket or bowl with intention – the idea is that it collects energy instead of letting it escape.
- ✓ A round mirror on the back of the door facing up the stairs can also help "bounce" prosperity back into your home.

With a few mindful tweaks, the stairs stop running you down and start supporting you. Energy flows better, you feel better, and your home starts to work with you instead of against you.

Chapter 6

Your Home Lifeline

Go back to your Magnetic Game Board. Do you see where the X marks the very center of your home? Now, draw a straight line through the center of the X parallel to the front door – from the Family area on one side, through Health in the middle, to Children & Creativity on the other. That line represents the lifeline of your home with a back half and a front half.

The Lifeline

Some rooms and features are best in the *back half of the home*: your kitchen, your stove, your dining room table, and your master bedroom. These are the rooms that nourish, restore, and ground you. They belong in a place of support and protection.

Other rooms are better suited to the *front half of the home:* a sitting room/library, an office and a guest room are great towards the front of the house.

Dining Rooms

Where You Nourish Yourself

Your dining table is sacred. It represents abundance, health, and the way you receive nourishment – physically, emotionally, and spiritually. It's where family gathers, where conversations flow, and where prosperity has a chance to settle in your home.

But here's the thing: when your dining room or dining table sits near the front door, that sacred energy can feel exposed, rushed, and unsettled. The front door is the main entry point for life force energy. If the table is right there in plain sight, the chi doesn't linger. It rushes past, and meals may feel less grounding, less connected, and less abundant.

It's no wonder that so many people with formal dining rooms in the front of their home rarely use them. Often, they turn into offices, storage areas, or a catch-all for clutter. I turned my dining area into an office that could be used as a dining table as needed. During Thanksgiving, when I sat in my front dining room, it felt uncomfortable, like I couldn't relax. I much preferred being in the kitchen or out back on the porch, where the energy felt safe and supportive.

The Difference Placement Makes

When the dining room is tucked into the back of the home, everything changes. In the back, you feel protected and able to let your guard down. The energy is quieter, more nurturing. Meals stretch longer, laughter deepens, and the food itself seems more nourishing because you can soak it in.

How to Ground and Protect Your Dining Room

If your dining table sits near the front door or can be seen from the front door, don't worry – there are ways to stabilize the energy:

- ✓ **Buffer the view.** Use a console, screen, or tall plant so the table isn't directly visible from the door.
- ✓ **Anchor with intention.** A rug under the table, a wooden surface, or a meaningful centerpiece (like a bowl of fruit, a candle, or fresh flowers) invites chi to linger.
- ✓ **Set the mood.** Use warm lighting, art, or mirrors that reflect abundance and togetherness.
- ✓ **Symbolize plenty.** Add a fruit bowl, crystal, or vase of flowers to radiate prosperity energy.
- ✓ **Move your dining room to the back of the home (energetically.)** Place a round mirror in the back half of your home so that it reflects the table which in essence moves it. This works for the stove and kitchen too.

Dining Room

Do's & Don'ts

DO:

- ✓ Place the dining room toward the back of the house, if possible, where energy feels grounded and safe.
- ✓ Anchor the table with a centerpiece, rug, or grounding décor to help chi stay and settle.
- ✓ Keep the space well-lit and inviting – soft lighting nurtures connection and warmth.
- ✓ Display symbols of abundance, like fruit, flowers, or meaningful artwork, to amplify prosperity energy.
- ✓ Use the dining table for meals and gatherings – it's meant to be enjoyed, not ignored.

DON'T:

- ✗ Position the dining table directly in sight of the front door – chi will rush out instead of nourishing your family.
- ✗ Let the table become a dumping ground for clutter – it blocks energy and connection.
- ✗ Choose harsh lighting or overly cold colors – these can make meals feel rushed or joyless.
- ✗ Use lonely or barren imagery in this space – it subconsciously limits abundance and connection.
- ✗ Forget intention – the dining room flourishes when you consciously treat it as sacred.

Think of your dining room as the heart of abundance in your home. When positioned and energized with care, it becomes more than a place to eat – it transforms into a sanctuary of nourishment, prosperity, and love.

The Master Bedroom

Your Soul's Sanctuary

I'll never forget walking into a consultation with a woman who said, "Tonja, I just don't sleep well, neither does my husband. I've tried everything – herbal teas, new mattresses, even white-noise machines. Nothing works."

Her bedroom was gorgeous, straight out of a design magazine. Plush pillows, elegant drapery, soothing colors. But the moment I stepped into the room, my feng shui radar went off.

The bed? Plunked right in line with the door. A desk covered in bills and work papers was pressed against the opposite wall. It was the first thing she saw when she woke up in the morning and the last thing she saw at night reminding her of work that needed to be done. Oh, and there was a full-length mirror facing directly at the bed, doubling every ounce of restless energy.

It didn't matter how beautiful it looked. Energetically, her "sanctuary" was keeping her mind working overtime.

We made a few simple shifts – moved the bed into command position, traded her desk for a couch upstairs which also gave her an awesome designated workspace. (Work has no business in your bedroom. Neither does exercise equipment.) We also moved the mirror away from her sleeping area. Within a week she called me: "Tonja, I don't know what you did, but I've slept better this week than I have in five years!"

Feng shui is not just about having pretty design. It's about aligning your energy with sanctuary, safety, and love.

Create Your Temple

Your bedroom is not just four walls and a bed – it is your most sacred sanctuary. This is the place where your body restores itself, where dreams are born, and where love and intimacy deepen. Nearly one-third of your life is spent here, which makes it the single most important space to nurture with intention.

When you treat your bedroom as a temple, you gather energy each night that fuels your health, your relationships, and your dreams. Rest becomes deeper, love rises more naturally, and your spirit feels fully held. The energy of this space ripples into every other part of your life.

Think of your bedroom as your cocoon – the sacred space where you recharge. If your home is a living, breathing reflection of your soul, then the bedroom is your soul's private temple. How you set it up influences everything: how rested you feel, how love shows up in your life, and how deeply your spirit can replenish. When the energy is off, you feel it. When the energy is aligned, it feels calm, safe, and magnetic.

The Essentials of a Magnetic Bedroom

Bed in Command Position

Place your bed so you can see the door without being directly in line with it. This calms your nervous system, signaling safety. When your body feels secure, your rest deepens.

Twin Nightstands

Two balanced nightstands represent equality and partnership. Even if you are single, they prepare and hold the energy for love to arrive.

Clutter-Free Energy Flow

Clear everything stored under the bed. Chi flows around you while you sleep like a gentle river. Old suitcases or clutter block that flow and weigh on you more than you realize.

Soothing Décor

Let your room whisper sanctuary. Choose soft colors, gentle textures, and artwork that inspires love and peace. Remember, the last thing you see before drifting into sleep and the first thing you see upon waking imprints on your soul.

Avoid Heavy, Looming Furniture

If a bookcase, mirror, or heavy artwork hangs above your bed or could fall toward you, move it. Even subconsciously, the sense of weight disturbs your deep rest.

The Sacred Position of the Bedroom

The master bedroom should always occupy the command position of the home – furthest from the front door, ideally at the back. If a bedroom is located in an extension at the front of the house, use that room for guests or an office. A child placed there may feel vulnerable or disconnected from the family, while guests will feel welcome but not inclined to overstay.

Your bedroom is your temple. With just a few mindful adjustments, you can transform it into the most magnetic space in your home – one that restores your body, nurtures your relationships, and supports the life you are creating.

Why Closing Your Bedroom Door Matters

Most people don't realize this: when you leave your bedroom door open, your energy drifts. In feng shui, doors are powerful – they're portals for chi. They invite it in, but they also let it slip away. If you have an ensuite bathroom, that energy can literally drain during the night unless the door to the bathroom is closed.

When you shut your bedroom door, you create a sacred container. Your energy gathers, stays with you, and strengthens while you rest. For couples, it deepens intimacy – holding your shared light close. For individuals, it becomes a boundary of self-respect and safety, a signal to your subconscious that this space is yours alone to restore and renew.

Want to amplify the effect? Place a round-faceted crystal above your bed or just inside the doorway. Add a beautiful charm, a soft chime, or even a simple symbol of peace. Each time you close the door, you're not just blocking noise or light — you're choosing to call your energy back, to center it, to let your bedroom hold it safe.

Closing the door is a ritual, a whisper to yourself and the universe: *this is my sanctuary, my protection, my place of rest and love.*

Bedroom "Don'ts"

To really create sanctuary, avoid these common energy leaks that steal your rest:

- ✕ **Mirrors Facing the Bed:** They double energy and stir restlessness (and can symbolically invite a "third party" into relationships.)
- ✕ **Electronics:** Screens and devices keep your energy "on." Cover them if they must stay. Better yet, put them in another room for the night.
- ✕ **Work in the Bedroom:** Desks and piles of paperwork scream *unfinished business.* Keep them out of your bedroom or divide the space if you must and add a screen in between your work area and where you sleep.
- ✕ **Clutter Under the Bed:** Heavy energy while you sleep equals heavy energy when you wake. Clear it. It also blocks energy flow.
- ✕ **Overly Yang Décor:** Yang is bold, yin is soft. Bright reds, harsh lighting, and busy patterns overstimulate your senses making sleep difficult. Choose soft, yin tones and textures.

× **Lonely or Sad Imagery:** Your subconscious soaks it in. Replace with calming nature scenes, positive messages, a vision board or imagery that represents what you want to call in.

× **Feet Aligned with the Door:** It's referred to as the coffin position because that is how they carried the dead out the door in ancient times. You want to see the door but be to the left or right of the doorway as you sleep. Energy flows out. If you can't move the bed, soften it with a round rug, place a piece of furniture at the foot of the bed or a round faceted crystal hanging from the ceiling between the bed and the doorway.

Chapter 7

The Command Position

The command position is located in an area furthest from the front door or an area of a room where you can see the doorway. Sitting with your back to a door doesn't feel safe and secure. If you have a choice of where you sit to eat, choose a seat in the back of your home (or the back of a restaurant) where you can see the door. You will feel more calm and relaxed which is important when you are taking in nourishment.

In your bedroom, this means having your bed placed so you can see the doorway without being directly in line with it – ideally in the back half of your home. This gives you a sense of solid footing in life, like you're truly in charge of your world.

When you're standing at your stove cooking, the same principle applies. You don't want your back to an entryway where energy (or people!) can sneak up behind you. Instead, you want to feel supported and aware. The stove is sacred – it's where you prepare the food that nourishes your body and family. That's why you don't want heavy cabinets looming directly over it. Your best energy should go into what you're creating.

If your stove isn't in the back half of the house, don't worry! One simple adjustment is to hang a mirror so you can see yourself reflected while you cook. This trick energetically "pulls" the stove's presence to the back of the house, as if your energy exists in both places.

Placement is power. Put the rooms that restore you in the back, the work that connects you in the front, and always honor the command position so you feel strong, supported, and fully in charge of your life.

A STORY

Who's in Charge Here?

I was in a strategy session with an executive coaching client. She shared that she was having challenges with one of her employees. Her assistant was showing up late, taking too much vacation time, not there when she was needed most, and even adding hours she didn't work to her timesheet.

Immediately, I recognized it as a command position issue. I asked her to draw her office layout on a piece of paper. Sure enough, they shared the same office sitting at one large desk. The employee was sitting on one side in the command position while my client had taken the submissive seat – back to the door--on the other side of the desk.

You might not think this matters, but it tells a story. It was an energetic standoff between them. When I asked why she set up her office that way, she admitted she liked the view – it looked out at the garden. Again, that tells a story: she wasn't prioritizing work, and subconsciously, she was avoiding taking control of the business dynamics.

I then went to the front door and observed what it would feel like from the perspective of a client walking in to meet and begin their design process. What do they see and feel?

Right at the front door, a large tree blocked the energy. She could have used wind chimes or a mirror to shift energy, but she chose to remove and relocate the tree, creating openness and flow. Inside, the space felt cluttered – not because it was messy, but because there was no clear focal point. A large printer was grabbing much of the attention. We moved the printer to the owner's office, where it was more functional and less distracting. Then created a more aesthetically pleasing focal point.

In another office, the associate had her desk against the wall. While it can make a room feel bigger, facing right into a wall like that blocks vision and stifles creativity. Working with your back to the door lowers productivity and drains vital energy. The moment we moved her desk to the command position so she could see the entrance, she felt an immediate lift. I could see it in her energy.

"I would never position a client's office up against a wall," she said. "I don't know why I did that for myself. It feels so much better now."

Recently, I watched a decluttering show on Netflix that featured a business owner struggling to stay focused while working from home. To help, the consultant installed a long built-in desk and shelves across an entire wall, creating an impressive amount of workspace and organization. On the surface, it looked like a perfect solution.

But there was a problem. Sitting at her desk, the owner's back was to the doorway. This may not seem like much, but energetically it makes a huge difference. Without the support of a wall behind her, she lacked a sense of stability. Subconsciously, her attention was pulled toward the possibility of someone approaching from behind. That constant low-level distraction keeps the nervous system on alert and drains focus.

Even more importantly, this position blocked her ability to clearly envision growth. Facing so close to the wall subtly limited her vision, which was especially concerning since her family was depending on her business success.

While the larger desk surface and vertical organization were valuable upgrades, the placement of her workspace was out of alignment with her intention. A more empowered desk position

– one where she could see the door and feel supported – would have amplified her focus and given her work greater importance.

In situations where moving the desk isn't possible, there are still adjustments that help. A high-backed chair can create a sense of protection, and a mirror placed on the shelves can reflect the doorway into her line of sight. These simple shifts calm the nervous system, restore focus, and allow her energy to flow into her business with more confidence.

Chapter 8

Your Front Door:

The Mouth of Chi

Your front door is your home's most powerful portal. In feng shui, it's called the *Mouth of Chi* – the place where energy enters your life. It's the first impression the universe gets of you, and its condition directly influences the quality of opportunities, prosperity, relationships, and abundance that flow into your home and into your life.

Wait – You Never Use Your Front Door?

If you usually enter through a garage or side door, you're unintentionally sending energy out the back. All jokes aside, neglecting the front door blocks the good juju from finding you. Make a practice of using your front door at least once a week. Open it wide, sweep the porch, straighten the mat, and see yourself sweeping out the old and inviting in fresh, vibrant energy. Your intention is the most powerful adjustment you can make, hold it in your mind with every action you take.

Pathway and Presentation.

The walk to your door matters. A gently curving path allows energy to gather and meander gracefully into your home. A long, straight path pointing like an arrow at the door can rush energy, creating tension or urgency. Good lighting acts like a beacon, drawing supportive energy in even after dark.

Your door itself should feel strong, welcoming, and maintained. Solid construction symbolizes stability and protection. Large, healthy plants on either side can enhance the flow of energy and create a warm invitation. Keep the area free of clutter, sweep the entryway, and place a wide, inviting welcome mat. Whether it says "welcome" or simply radiates warmth, it signals to the universe: *I'm ready to receive.*

Colors Speak Energy

The color of your door amplifies its intention:

- ✓ **Red:** Prosperity, recognition, protection
- ✓ **Black:** Wisdom, flow, clarity
- ✓ **Green:** Growth, renewal, vitality
- ✓ **Blue:** Calm, trust, communication
- ✓ **White:** Clarity, fresh beginnings
- ✓ **Yellow/Earth Tones:** Grounding, support, stability

Paint it a color that stands out from the rest of your home and don't paint any other doors (including the garage door) the same color. Choose a color you love that makes you feel great and add a drop of that awesome Magnetic Home Red Polish to it. Mix it in, stirring in your good intentions for abundance, health and harmony with it.

Two or More Front Doors

Have you ever gone up to a house that had two front doors? I have and I didn't know which was the main door. I stood there for a bit, hesitant, afraid I might go to the wrong door. Well, if you have two or more doors, energy works in the same way. It doesn't know which door is the main one, so it just sits and waits without going inside. You need to send a clear signal.

If your home has two or more doors – perhaps a formal entrance and a functional everyday door – choose the one that best aligns with your intentions for flow and energy. Treat both as important portals but prioritize and designate one your front door. Paint it a different color than the house. Make sure your house number is by your designated front door. Keep the pathway clear, clean, and visually welcoming. The other door should be painted the same color as the house so as not confuse the energy (or anyone coming to your home.)

Garage Door Entrances

If you mainly enter through a garage, it's okay, but it shouldn't be your only doorway. The garage door is functional, not magnetic. Make a point to step through your front door regularly to activate the energy flow, bringing positive energy into your home. Even small gestures – opening it, sweeping, placing a plant nearby – reinforce your intention to receive life's blessings.

Unlike Narnia: When Hidden Doors Aren't Magical

If your front door is tucked away, recessed, or otherwise easy to miss, it can signal good things aren't making their way to you. Don't worry – you can still call in the good lifeforce energy. Add a cheerful wind chime to announce the entrance, or a bright welcome flag or decorative sign to guide energy and guests alike. Pathway lighting, potted plants, or a small water feature can help draw attention and encourage chi to flow naturally toward the door. The goal is to make the entrance visible, inviting, and unmistakably welcoming – so that both energy and visitors know exactly where to come, and your home can receive all the abundance, opportunities, and connection it's ready for.

Additional Enhancements

- ✓ Add a faceted crystal above the door to disperse stagnant energy and bring sparkle to the entry.
- ✓ Keep the lighting warm and inviting to create a safe, welcoming feeling.
- ✓ A clean, clutter-free interior entry signals readiness for opportunity and prosperity.
- ✓ Make sure your house numbers are near the front door. This calls in the beneficial energy.

Your front door is more than a physical entry – it's your energetic threshold. Use it consciously. Sweep, polish, plant, open, and invite. By treating it with intention, you create a magnet for wealth, love, opportunities, and all the magic you want flowing into your life.

Chapter 9

Let's Play!

Making Your Moves on the Magnetic Dream Board

Before we begin, I invite you to pause and appreciate what is already present in your life. The truth is you are successful in many ways. In fact, I would bet that you've experienced at least some success in each of the Nine Life Areas.

Because we are wired to grow and evolve, it's natural to focus on what's next, forgetting all about what we've accomplished to get to where we are in this moment. That drive can sometimes blur our perception of success of all that we have already done well.

What we focus on expands. Too often, our energy goes toward what isn't working rather than what is. Yet manifesting begins by shifting into a high vibration—and gratitude is one of the highest frequencies we can hold.

Celebrate Your Success

When you celebrate your success, even the small ones, you amplify your magnetic field. The universe responds to gratitude like a tuning fork, sending more of what you appreciate directly back to you. This simple act of acknowledgment brings you into alignment with joy, clarity, and flow.

Gratitude raises your vibration and opens the channel for abundance. Let this be your starting point.

Use these prompts to anchor yourself in appreciation and celebration. Write freely, without judgment – let your wins, big or small, be seen and honored.

Three things I am most grateful for right now are:

1. _____

2. _____

3. _____

A recent success or breakthrough I've experienced is:

_____

_____

_____

Something in my home or environment that already supports me is:

_____

_____

One way I've grown in the past year is:

_____

_____

I feel proud of myself for:

_____

_____

reflect _____

Take a moment to honor what is already working beautifully in your life. Breathe deeply. Place your hand on your heart. Feel thankful for the blessings you've received, the progress you've made, the people who support you, and the opportunities that have already come your way. Say out loud, "I celebrate my successes with joy and gratitude. I honor how far I've come and open my heart to receive even more blessings."

Making Enhancements in the Life Areas

Go back to page 47 and look at what three life areas you want to change first and write your intention for each one. I've included some samples of intentions for you or keep the ones you have.

Life Area   /   Your Intention(s)

1._____

2._____

3._____

Sample Intentions

Prosperity

- ✓ To receive $500 Million to build a power plant.
- ✓ To receive $10,000 or more into my savings account.
- ✓ To increase my net worth.
- ✓ To attract consistent financial growth.
- ✓ To manage resources wisely and effectively.

Fame & Reputation

- ✓ To receive recognition for my contributions.
- ✓ To be seen and appreciated for my talents.
- ✓ To step confidently into my leadership.
- ✓ To build credibility and trust in my work.
- ✓ To shine authentically in my community.

Partnership

- ✓ To attract a loving and supportive partner.
- ✓ To improve harmony with my business partner.
- ✓ To deepen trust and communication with my romantic partner.
- ✓ To feel emotionally fulfilled in my relationships.
- ✓ To nurture partnerships that align with my values.

Family of Origin

- ✓ To strengthen bonds with my brother, mother, etc.
- ✓ To create harmony and peace regarding an inheritance.
- ✓ To feel supported as I start in a new direction.
- ✓ To resolve conflicts with clarity and love.
- ✓ To heal ancestral trauma.

Health

- ✓ To maintain vibrant energy and vitality.
- ✓ To make healthy choices for my body and mind.
- ✓ To reduce stress and feel balanced daily.
- ✓ To support my overall wellness naturally.
- ✓ To increase my physical and emotional resilience.

Children & Creativity

- ✓ To express my creativity freely.
- ✓ To successfully launch my book project.
- ✓ To bring joy and play into my daily life.
- ✓ To support my children.
- ✓ To encourage curiosity and imagination in myself and others.

Knowledge & Wisdom

- ✓ To gain clarity about myself and my choices.
- ✓ To get As and Bs in school.
- ✓ To deepen my understanding of life and myself.
- ✓ To reflect and grow wiser from experiences.
- ✓ To expand my perspective and intuition daily.

Career

- ✓ To be promoted at work.
- ✓ To figure out my life path and purpose.
- ✓ To make choices that support my growth.
- ✓ To trust my intuition in major decisions.
- ✓ To feel clarity and focus in my journey.

Helpful People/Travel

- ✓ To connect with supportive and inspiring people.
- ✓ To receive guidance or mentorship when needed.

✓ To travel or experience new opportunities for growth.
✓ To build a network that helps me thrive.
✓ To attract collaborations that align with my goals.

Giving Energy to Your Intentions.

Choose up to three adjustments in the three life areas you most want to enhance. Every life area comes with its own "game pieces" you can choose to play with – color, element, shape(s), number, family member, and natural element.

Before making changes, always clear any clutter or fix anything broken in the area, holding your intention as you do so. If there are challenges such as bathrooms, stairs, or missing parts of the floor plan, those should be adjusted as well. See previous chapters.

Here's the most important rule: don't over-adjust. Making too many changes scatters the energy. One powerful, intentional adjustment can be more effective than many small ones.

My feng shui teacher explained it like this: imagine you want a can of soup, so you send ten people to the store. At the grocery store, they bump into each other, realize they're all there for the same can of soup, and each assumes someone else will get it. In the end, nobody buys the soup.

One clear request. One to three subtle adjustments. That's how you get results. Here are the ways to adjust each area:

Prosperity

Description: This area governs abundance in all its forms – not only money, but also blessings, opportunities, and a sense of richness in life. It represents royalty, thus the color purple. When balanced, it radiates gratitude, generosity, and the ability to receive.

Color: Purple

Element: Wood (Water most often used because water feeds wood.)
Shapes: Rectangles, Vertical Lines
Natural Element: Wind
This area also represents: Hips, legs, feet and the oldest daughter

Affirmations:

- Money flows easily and abundantly to me.
- I receive new financial opportunities and prosperity.
- I receive $5,000 or more per month.

The Prosperity area thrives on wood energy – plants, upward growth, green and purple colors – supported by a touch of water to keep that growth nourished. The key is vitality, flow, and expansion.

Challenges in the Prosperity Area

✓ **Fireplaces:** Fire burns up wealth energy.
  ○ **Adjustment:** Place a mirror above the fireplace to symbolically keep the wealth energy circulating, or use a plant/wood element nearby to feed the fire productively.
✓ **Bathrooms / Toilets:** Drains can pull prosperity energy down and out.
  ○ **Adjustment**: Keep toilet lids closed, use red tape or marker around drains, or place a healthy plant to draw from the water and transform the energy.
✓ **Clutter or Storage Rooms:** Stuck energy in the prosperity corner equals stuck finances.
  ○ **Adjustment:** Clear out clutter, organize the space, and add a symbol of growth such as a thriving plant.
✓ **Kitchens (especially stoves in this corner):** Kitchen energy can "burn" wealth if not balanced.

- **Adjustment:** Use wood elements such as plants, green accents, or tall shapes to mediate fire, and mirrors to symbolically double the burners, representing doubling prosperity.
- ✓ **Empty or Missing Corner:** If the prosperity corner of the home is cut off, prosperity energy can feel weak. Watch for missing corners in a room as well.
  - **Adjustment:** Use landscaping outside, mirrors, or symbolic objects such as a flag or light to call in the missing energy.
- ✓ **Overuse of Fire Colors:** Too much fire element here can burn away wealth instead of fueling it.
  - **Adjustment:** Balance with wood – plants, green tones, or tall vertical shapes – to feed the fire in a natural and productive way.
- ✓ **Dead or Dying Plants:** Since prosperity is a wood area, dead plants symbolize blocked or declining growth.
  - **Adjustment:** Replace with thriving plants. Bamboo and money trees are particularly beneficial in this area.

Example: Adjusting for Prosperity

If I wanted to increase my prosperity, I would first look at what's happening in the Prosperity Area of my home. Suppose I discover that my bathroom is in the prosperity area.

Here are some adjustments I might make:

- ✓ Place a plant or a bowl of rice on the back of the toilet, holding the intention that water rises to feed the plant.
- ✓ Use a red marker to outline the drain in the tub, setting the intention that prosperity is overflowing in my life. Do the same with the bathroom sink drain.
- ✓ Write a positive affirmation in purple marker, tuck the paper into the plant, and use the Three Secrets of Reinforcement to anchor it.

- ✓ Write a prosperity check to myself and place it in the prosperity corner of my desk.
- ✓ Add a water feature in the Prosperity Area of my garden.

note

If you use a feature like a plant or water fountain, keep it healthy and active. If a plant dies, replace it with something even better. Not every adjustment needs to be seen. You can tuck pictures in a plant like I did in my bathroom, or you can place items under a couch, behind a piece of artwork, etc. Be creative.

Fame & Reputation

Description: This area is about your good name, your light in the world – how others see you, your integrity, and the legacy you leave behind. It's about recognition, confidence, and being seen authentically for who you are.

Colors: Red
Element: Fire
Shapes: Triangles, pointed forms like pyramids
Natural Element: Fire
This area also represents: Face, eyes, and the middle daughter
Enhancements: The color red, triangles, and pyramids. Candles. Use your awards, certificates, symbolic objects, red accents or candles, clean and organized space.

Affirmations:

- I shine my light with confidence, and my work is seen and appreciated.
- I step into my authority and am respected for my contributions.
- Recognition flows to me naturally and effortlessly.

The Fame & Reputation area thrives on fire energy – bright light, recognition, passion, and expansion. The colors here are red, orange, and strong warm tones, supported by wood to fuel the fire. The keys are visibility, illumination, and clarity of purpose.

Challenges in the Fame & Reputation Area

✓ **Fireplaces or Overpowering Fire:** While this area is naturally fire, too much can burn out recognition or create conflict.

  ○ **Adjustment:** Balance with wood elements such as plants, or introduce earth (square shapes, pottery, yellow/brown tones) to ground the excess fire.

✓ **Bathrooms/Toilets:** Drains here can wash away reputation and recognition.

  ○ **Adjustment:** Keep the toilet lid closed, use red tape or marker around drains, or place a mirror on the outside of the bathroom door to symbolically contain energy.

✓ **Clutter or Dark Corners:** Darkness or mess in this area dims your visibility and personal fire.

  ○ **Adjustment:** Add bright lighting, lamps, or candles. Clear clutter and allow energy to flow freely.

✓ **Mirrors Facing Each Other or Facing the Door:** Too many reflections scatter energy, creating confusion about how you are seen.

  ○ **Adjustment:** Limit or reposition mirrors to avoid energy "bouncing" away.

✓ **Missing Corner:** If the Fame & Reputation area is cut off, your recognition and visibility can be weakened.

  ○ **Adjustment:** Use lights outside, flags, plants, or mirrors to symbolically call back the missing energy.

✓ **Water Features** Since water puts out fire, too much water here can dampen your shine.

    o **Adjustment:** Balance with candles, lamps, or red décor to reignite the energy.

Example: Adjusting for Fame & Reputation

If I wanted to strengthen my reputation and be more recognized for my work, I would look at what is happening in the Fame & Reputation area of my home. Suppose I discover that the space is dark and cluttered.

Here are some adjustments I might make:

- ✓ Place a bright lamp in the Fame & Reputation corner to illuminate my path and intentions.
- ✓ Add red candles or artwork featuring the color red to fuel the fire element.
- ✓ Write an affirmation such as "I am seen, valued, and appreciated for who I am" and place it under a candle. Add a healthy plant to feed the fire with wood energy.
- ✓ If it's outdoors, I might plant red flowers or place a light that shines upward at night to call in visibility and recognition.

Partnership

Description: Reflects love, romance, and deep connections. Supports harmony, communication, and mutual support in relationships – romantic, business, or friendship.

Colors: Pink, mauve (avoid peach or apricot)
Element: Earth (Fire supports earth)
Shapes: Squares, rectangles, flat
Natural Element: Earth
This area also represents: Abdomen and the mother
Enhancements: Objects in pairs (candles, crystals, décor), love-themed artwork or photos, tidy and intentional space.

Affirmations:

- I attract loving, supportive relationships into my life.

- My heart is open to love, and I nurture connection.
- I welcome harmonious and balanced partnerships.

The Partnerships area thrives on earth energy – grounding, stability, love, and harmony. The colors here are pink, white, and soft tones. Shapes are square (earth) and sometimes paired items to symbolize balance. The key is unity, trust, and supportive relationships.

Challenges in the Partnership Area

✓ **Bathrooms/Toilets:** Energy can "flush away" harmony and intimacy.
  - **Adjustment:** Keep lids closed, use red tape or marker around drains, and place pairs of objects (candles, vases, or crystals) to symbolize supportive partnership.

✓ **Clutter or Storage:** Stagnant energy here may show up as confusion in relationships.
  - **Adjustment:** Clear clutter and intentionally place symbols of love – such as paired items, meaningful photos, or rose quartz.

✓ **Single Items:** A single chair, lone artwork, or isolated symbol can reflect loneliness.
  - **Adjustment:** Add things in pairs to anchor togetherness.

✓ **Sharp Angles or Harsh Décor:** Pointed or aggressive shapes create conflict energy.
  - **Adjustment:** Use soft textures, rounded shapes, and soothing colors.

✓ **Missing Corner:** When this area is missing, relationships may feel unstable.
  - **Adjustment:** Use plants, lighting, or artwork outside to symbolically "complete" the corner.

Example: Adjusting for Partnerships

If I wanted to attract a supportive partner or strengthen my marriage, I would look at what is happening in the Partnership area of my home and my bedroom.

Here are some adjustments I might make:

- ✓ Place two candles on a shelf with the intention of shared warmth and light.
- ✓ Add rose quartz crystals in pairs to symbolize love.
- ✓ Keep the space clean and serene, with soft pinks and whites.
- ✓ Write an affirmation like "I welcome love and harmony into my life." and tuck it under a pair of objects.

Family of Origin

Description: Honors roots, ancestry, and the support systems that ground you. Reflects loyalty, unity, and drawing strength from family and heritage.

Colors: Green, brown, earthy tones
Element: Wood
Shapes: Rectangles, vertical forms
Natural Element: Thunder
This area also represents: Spine, back, and parents, grandparents, aunts, uncles and extended family
Enhancements: Put family photos in a green picture frame and place in the family area, place heirlooms and plants in the area.

Affirmations:

- My family is connected, supported, and harmonious.
- I am grounded and secure in my family life.
- Love, understanding, and stability flow through my home.

The Family of Origin area thrives on wood energy – growth, strength, vitality, and ancestry. Its color is green, with tall rectangular shapes. The key is rootedness, resilience, and healthy beginnings.

Challenges in the Family of Origin Area

✓ **Bathrooms/Toilets**
Energy drains can weaken family bonds or health.
   o **Adjustment:** Use plants to draw water upward, or red tape/marker around drains.
✓ **Broken Items or Dead Plants:** Symbolizes broken ties or declining health.
   o **Adjustment:** Repair, replace, or remove anything that is damaged or lifeless.
✓ **Clutter:** Stuck energy here creates tension in family dynamics.
   o **Adjustment:** Clear and organize the space, add thriving plants or wood elements.
✓ **Missing Corner:** A cut-off Family of Origin area can weaken support systems.
   o **Adjustment:** Use outdoor landscaping, trees, or symbolic items like wind chimes to strengthen this energy.
✓ **Overuse of Metal:** Metal cuts wood, so too much metal weakens family support.
   o **Adjustment:** Balance with wood (plants, tall shapes) and a touch of water to feed growth.

Example: Adjusting for Family of Origin

If I wanted to strengthen my family bonds, I would look at what is happening in the Family of Origin area of my home.

Here are some adjustments I might make:

✓ Replace a dead plant with a thriving one.
✓ Add a framed photo of my family in a wooden frame.
✓ Write an affirmation like "My family is strong, supportive, and thriving" and place it under a plant.

Health

Description: The heart of the home, influencing vitality, balance, and overall well-being. Harmonizes body, mind, and spirit.

Colors: Yellow, earth tones
Element: Earth
Shapes: Squares, rectangles, flat
Natural Element: The Universe
This area also represents: Heart, stomach, digestive system and self or caregiver
Enhancements: Open, clutter-free space, grounding items (crystals, round rug), soft warm lighting.

Affirmations:

- I am vibrant, healthy, and balanced in mind, body, and spirit.
- Energy, vitality, and well-being flow through me freely.
- I am grounded, centered, and whole.

The Health Area is the center of the Magnetic Game Board and touches all life areas. It thrives on earth energy – balance, grounding, and nourishment. Its colors are yellow, brown, and earthy tones, with square shapes. The keys are harmony, wholeness, and vitality.

Challenges in the Health Area

- ✓ **Clutter:** Stagnant energy in the center affects the entire home.
    - ○ **Adjustment:** Keep this area open, organized, and easy to move through.
- ✓ **Bathrooms or Drains** These can symbolize energy leaking out of overall health.
    - ○ **Adjustment:** Use plants, mirrors, or intention symbols to shift energy upward.

- ✓ **Missing Center (Open Floor Plan)** If the center of the home feels "hollow," vitality can feel weakened.
  - ○ **Adjustment:** Place a grounding rug, square table, or earth-tone art to anchor the space.
  - ○ **Broken or Worn Furniture:** Reflects wear on health. **Adjustment:** Repair or replace items, using sturdy, supportive pieces.
- ✓ **Low Lighting** Dimness here represents low vitality.
  - ○ **Adjustment:** Use warm lighting to brighten and balance.

Example: Adjusting for Health

If I wanted to improve my overall well-being, I would check the center of my home. Suppose I discover that it is cluttered with piles of items.

Here are some adjustments I might make:

- ✓ Clear out the space completely, allowing energy to flow.
- ✓ Place a grounding object like a square, earthy rug in warm colors.
- ✓ Add a ceramic bowl filled with fruit or stones as a symbol of nourishment.
- ✓ Write an affirmation like "I am vibrant, balanced, and full of health" and place it under the bowl.

Children & Creativity

Description: Governs joy, playfulness, imagination, and new beginnings – both literal children and creative projects.

Colors: White, pastels, light tones
Element: Metal
Shapes: Circles, ovals
Natural Element: Lake
This area also represents: Lungs, respiratory system, mouth and the youngest daughter, children, grandchildren, and mentees.

Enhancements: Art supplies, musical instruments, playful objects, organized but open space, light and cheerful colors.

Affirmations:

- Creativity flows freely, and inspiration comes effortlessly.
- New ideas and projects manifest with ease.
- I nurture creativity and growth in myself and others.

This area thrives on metal energy – joy, playfulness, creativity, and completion. Its colors are white, pastels, and metallics, with circular shapes. The keys are inspiration, imagination, and fun.

Challenges in the Children & Creativity Area

- ✓ **Bathrooms/Toilets:** Energy drains may suppress creativity or block joy.
  - ○ **Adjustment:** Use mirrors, intention symbols, or playful décor to shift energy.
- ✓ **Broken Toys or Art Supplies:** Symbolizes stalled or blocked creativity.
  - ○ **Adjustment:** Repair or replace with items that inspire joy.
- ✓ **Clutter:** Stagnant energy here blocks playful flow.
  - ○ **Adjustment:** Keep the area light, fresh, and open.
- ✓ **Missing Corner:** Can reduce the spark of creativity or delay new projects.
  - ○ **Adjustment:** Use outdoor décor, lights, or a symbolic circular item to complete it.
- ✓ **Overuse of Fire:** Too much fire here melts metal energy.
  - ○ **Adjustment:** Use white, metallics, or circles to strengthen.

Example: Adjusting for Creativity

If I wanted to feel more inspired in my work, I would check the Children & Creativity area.

Here are some adjustments I might make:

- ✓ Add artwork I love in a white or metallic frame.
- ✓ Place a circular bowl with colorful stones or marbles to symbolize playful energy.
- ✓ Write an affirmation like "I am inspired and my creativity flows with joy." and place it with my art supplies.

Knowledge & Wisdom

Description: Area of inner growth, wisdom, and spiritual insight. Supports meditation, study, and reflective clarity.

Colors: Blue, black, earthy tones
Element: Earth
Shapes: Squares, rectangles
Natural Element: Mountain
This area also represents: Hands and the youngest son
Enhancements: Books, journals, learning materials, inspiring quotes/art, soft bright lighting.

Affirmations:

- I expand my knowledge and wisdom every day.
- Insight, clarity, and understanding flow easily to me.
- I am guided by intelligence and intuition.

This area thrives on earth energy – stillness, wisdom, and inner clarity. Its colors are blue and earthy tones, with square shapes. The key is reflection, self-awareness, and grounded insight.

Challenges in the Knowledge & Wisdom Area

- ✓ **Bathrooms/Toilets:** Drains here can weaken self-awareness.
  - ○ **Adjustment:** Use red tape around drains or place intention objects like books or symbols of wisdom.
- ✓ **Clutter:** Clarity can't thrive in confusion.

- ○ **Adjustment:** Clear the space and add items that inspire stillness (cushions, books, or calming artwork).
- ✓ **Darkness:** Dim lighting represents foggy thinking.
  - ○ **Adjustment:** Use soft, steady lighting to encourage contemplation.
- ✓ **Missing Corner:** When absent, clarity may feel elusive.
  - ○ **Adjustment:** Use lights, stones, or grounded symbols outside to strengthen.
- ✓ **Overuse of Metal or Fire:** These can overpower earth's stability.
  - ○ **Adjustment:** Anchor with stones, pottery, or earthy objects.

Example: Adjusting for Knowledge & Wisdom

If I wanted more clarity, I would check the Knowledge & Wisdom area of my home. Suppose I find it dark and cluttered.

Here are some adjustments I might make:

- ✓ Add a lamp with warm, steady light.
- ✓ Place a meditation cushion or small altar here.
- ✓ Write an affirmation like "I know and trust myself deeply" and place it under a grounding stone.

Career

Description: Governs your career, purpose, and flow of opportunities. Encourages clarity, focus, and alignment with your highest calling.

Colors: Black, blue, dark tones
Element: Water
Shapes: Wavy, flowing, amorphous
Natural Element: River
This area also represents: Ears, kidneys and the Middle Son

Enhancements: Small fountain, water-themed art, clear desk, life-goal symbols Keep it open and uncluttered to invite clarity and flow into your professional life. A dark-colored rug, water element, or even an inspiring affirmation can strengthen this zone.

Affirmations:

- I move confidently on my life path, and new opportunities flow to me.
- I am clear, focused, and inspired in my choices.
- I attract the right people, projects, and circumstances to support my growth.

This area thrives on water energy – flow, movement, and purpose. Its colors are black and dark blues, with wavy or freeform shapes. The keys are career, calling, and life path.

Challenges in the Career Area

- ✓ **Bathrooms/Toilets:** Drains here can "drain away" opportunities.
  - ○ **Adjustment:** Close lids, use mirrors or plants to lift energy.
- ✓ **Clutter:** Stagnant energy here blocks career flow.
  - ○ **Adjustment:** Keep entryways and hallways clear, since this area is often near the front door.
- ✓ **Broken or Stuck Doors:** A front door that sticks, squeaks, or doesn't open fully symbolizes blocked opportunities.
  - ○ **Adjustment:** Repair the door, oil hinges, and make sure it opens freely.
- ✓ **Missing Corner:** Can lead to confusion about purpose.
  - ○ **Adjustment:** Use outdoor water features, lights, or symbolic items to strengthen.
- ✓ **Overuse of Earth:** Earth dams water, so too much can block flow.
  - ○ **Adjustment:** Add flowing shapes, mirrors, or water imagery.

Example: Adjusting for Career

If I wanted to feel more confident in my career, I would check the Career area. Suppose I find clutter by my front door.

Here are some adjustments I might make:
- ✓ Clear the entryway completely and make it inviting.
- ✓ Add a mirror or artwork with flowing water.
- ✓ Place a fountain or bowl of water as a symbol of flow.
- ✓ Write an affirmation like "My path is clear and I move forward with ease" and place it near the door.

Helpful People/Travel

Description: Governs mentors, guides, supportive relationships, and journeys. Invites divine assistance, collaboration, and adventure.

Colors: Grey
Element: Metal
Shapes: Circles, spheres
Natural Element: Heaven
This area also represents: Head and the father
Enhancements: Photos of mentors/partners, travel symbols, gratitude tokens, organized and uncluttered.

Affirmations:
- I attract supportive, inspiring people into my life.
- Guidance, mentorship, and collaboration flow to me easily.
- The universe opens doors for travel and expansion.

This area thrives on metal energy – support, connections, and new horizons. Its colors are gray, white, and metallic and circular shapes. The key is helpful relationships, mentors, and travel.

Challenges in the Helpful People Area

- ✓ **Bathrooms/Toilets:** Drains may pull away support or delay helpful connections.
  - ○ **Adjustment:** Use mirrors, intention symbols, or circular metallic items.
- ✓ **Clutter:** Stuck energy here can make you feel unsupported.
  - ○ **Adjustment:** Keep the space fresh, clean, and open.
- ✓ **Missing Corner:** A cut-off area may delay mentors or travel opportunities.
  - ○ **Adjustment:** Use lights, plants, or round metallic décor outside to strengthen.
- ✓ **Overuse of Fire:** Fire melts metal, weakening support.
  - ○ **Adjustment:** Balance with gray, white, or circular shapes.
- ✓ **Unused or Forgotten Spaces:** Neglect here can show up as feeling unsupported in life.
  - ○ **Adjustment:** Activate the space with meaningful travel items, maps, or photos of mentors.

Example: Adjusting for Helpful People/Travel

If I wanted to attract supportive mentors or begin to travel more, I would check the Helpful People/Travel area. Suppose I find it full of clutter.

Here are some adjustments I might make:

- ✓ Clear it out and keep it open.
- ✓ Place a round metallic bowl with the names of mentors I wish to call in.
- ✓ Add travel photos, a globe, or symbols of places I wish to visit in the next 18 months.
- ✓ Write an affirmation like "I am supported by helpful people everywhere I go." and tuck it into the bowl.

The Three Secrets of Reinforcement

Adding a Boost of Magic

Choose or create a game piece (crystal, object of a certain color, something you love, a piece of paper with an affirmation, etc.) inspired by that life area you are intending to shift. It will hold the energy of your intention. This game piece can be placed in the life area of your whole house, a single room like your bedroom or office, or even on a flat surface such as a desktop.

As you place the object, use the Three Secrets of Reinforcement:

1. **Hold the Intention Clearly** Hold your object and fully focus on what you wish to manifest. Visualize it, feel it, and hold it in your mind with clarity and certainty. Your intention is the seed that enhances the energy in that space.

2. **Say the Six True Words Nine Times** Place your hands in the calming heart mudra: one hand rests on top of the other, palms up, thumbs touching at navel height. Repeat the Six True Words – *Om Ma Ni Pad Me Hum* – nine times. This mantra tunes your vibration, aligns your energy with your intention, and amplifies the power of your adjustment.

3. **Place Your Object with Awareness** Finally, place the item you are using for the adjustment – a crystal, plant, symbol, or other object – mindfully in the designated area. As you do, visualize your intention

radiating through the object, anchoring your desire into the space.

When practiced together, these three steps transform your space into a magnetic home for your intentions, supporting your goals and elevating your vibration effortlessly.

Chapter 10

_____

Common Challenges

and What You Can Do

In feng shui, it is said that our lives are shaped by three kinds of luck: **Heaven Luck, Earth Luck, and Human Luck.** Although I had figured these out for myself and called these other things, this is a simple way to understand. Together, they create the flow of our destiny, yet each one gives us opportunities to grow, align, and co-create with the Universe. Our common challenges usually rise from Heaven Luck. The good news is that both Earth Luck and Human Luck offer everything we need to overcome Heaven Luck.

Heaven Luck.

This is the hand you were dealt when you were born – the circumstances of your birth, the area you were born, the family you were born into, your natural talents and gifts, and even the challenges that come up as part of your pre-chosen soul path. While you cannot do anything to change these circumstances, Heaven Luck reminds us that we each arrive with a soul purpose and unique gifts to fulfill our purpose.

Earth Luck

This is about the energy that surrounds you. This is the focus of Magnetic Home. The spaces you live and work in, the land beneath your feet, the home you chose, the energy flow within it and the people you choose to hang out with all contribute to your Earth Luck. You have the ability to create harmony in your surroundings and relationships so that you are supported rather than drained. By being aware of the outside influences around you, you invite more ease, opportunity, and abundance into your experience.

Human Luck

This is the luck you create through your actions, your choices, and your mindset. It is shaped by your thoughts, your intentions, your habits, and the way you treat others. When you cultivate clarity, kindness, and perseverance, your Human Luck expands. Doing things to enhance your personal energy like daily rituals, meditation, doing things you love and following through on inspired action all strengthen this kind of luck.

Human Luck and Earth Luck are two sides of the same coin.

Human Luck reflects your Earth Luck and your Earth Luck reflects your Human Luck Changing one changes the other. It's kind of like what came first: the chicken or the egg? It doesn't matter. They mirror each other.

Everyone has a natural born desire to feel the best they can. We are all seekers in that regard. Some of us really delve in and ask ourselves what we want and others don't know that's an option and they just keep driving offroad at 80 miles per hour complaining about all the bumps and potholes.

If we take the time to investigate and get clear on what it is we really want vs. complaining about what isn't working, providence will move with you to bring that to fruition.

It's time to ask yourself some important questions. What is it that you truly desire to experience in this life you have been given? If money was off the table, what else would be important to you?

Wishful thinking is like light particles. Burning desire is like the laser beam.

Don't even bother with pie-in-the-sky affirmations. Get real about who you are and what you want. There is no right or wrong. I suspect you are already way ahead of the game because you have chosen to go against the norm and live a life outside the box. It's why you are here.

Simply put – sometimes life happens. But the question is: what can we do about it? The answer is that we can adjust our environment and remember that we were also born with everything we need inside of us to master any situation.

First, look to yourself and do the mundane. Do the things you know to do but maybe have been procrastinating on. If you have money leaks, look at your monthly statements and cancel any recurring payments you don't need. Then, use feng shui cures like adjusting for bathrooms in the prosperity area.

I once worked with a woman who had incredible drive. She was talented, educated, and motivated, a shining example of strong Human Luck. Her family background had given her a sense of faith and timing (Heaven Luck). Yet despite all her effort, her business wasn't producing as much as she knew it could be.

When I visited her home, I immediately saw what was happening. Her office was tucked away in a back corner, barely enough room to move, her desk pushed against a wall with her back to the door. Her Prosperity area was cluttered with broken electronics, and the pathway to her front door was blocked by overgrown bushes.

We found a better location for her office area near the front door. We then made sure her desk was positioned in the command position, cleared her Prosperity corner, and opened her front entry making way for clients to show up, the energy shifted and so did hers. Within weeks, new clients began calling her, and she told me it felt as though "the universe had finally found her address."

Here are some common challenges:

Challenge: My savings account keeps dwindling even though I make good money.

Ask Yourself: Is this a lifestyle issue? Did something change and you haven't adjusted your financial plan? Or do unexpected things keep happening?

Possible Feng Shui Causes:
- ✓ Leaks in the home or on your property. Fix leaky faucets or toilets ASAP!
- ✓ A staircase leading to the front door, if so, add a round mirror (it can be teeny-tiny) to the back of the front door facing the stairs reversing the flow or add a round rug between the front door and the staircase to pool the flow or add a money basket near the front door.
- ✓ The property lacks support in the Prosperity area or has a big slope draining money energy away. Plant a tree or trees to bring the supportive prosperity energy up or use a landscape light to energetically push the energy up in that area.

Check the Prosperity Area:
- ✓ Clutter: Get that mindfully cleared and organized. You could use purple folders for extra energy.

- ✓ Bathroom: Correct for the energy drain that comes with bathrooms and fix any leaky faucets.
- ✓ Fireplace in the area: Fire burns wood and the prosperity is a wood element so the energy is going up in smoke. Add a water element (something black, a picture of water, something with wavy lines, etc.) on or near the fireplace to dampen the fire energy

Mundane Solutions:

- ✓ Look through your monthly bank and credit card statements and intentionally stop any money leaks by cancelling any subscriptions you don't need.
- ✓ If something is putting a drain on your finances, i.e. credit card debt, a property you own, etc. write down all the ways that you could resolve this situation, sell the property, downsize, restructure your debt, etc.

Affirmation: "I feel good that my savings account is growing each month."

Challenge: I'm not sleeping well at night.

Ask Yourself: Has this been going on for a long time? Or did something change recently?

Good sleep is everything. It is how we recharge mentally, physically and spiritually; go to the astral plane at night to receive support in fulfilling our intentions and visions through ideas, helpful people, etc. Bedrooms are for sleeping. Period.

Possible Feng Shui Causes:

- ✓ The bedroom is too chaotic: Your bedroom should have the look and feel of a serene, soft hotel room minus the television.
    - o No tall bookshelves or heavy objects/artwork above the bed. Subconsciously you are on guard in case they fall.

- Remove any vibrant or aggressive artwork, instead calming picturesque views in greens and blues representing nature and the ocean. Add plants and more natural elements.
- Mirrors: If visible from your bed, they should be removed or covered at night.
- Televisions and electronics: This is a tough one, but remove any electronics from the room, including your cell phone. When you go to bed at night, put your cellphone in another room.
- Exercise equipment and/or work desks: Remove these items and don't do any work in the bedroom. If you must have it in the bedroom, intentionally block it from the bedroom with a screen or by putting a cloth over it at night.

✓ Bed improperly positioned: Move your bed to the command position on a solid wall with a solid headboard (no metal), assuring your feet are not pointing directly out the doorway. Make sure no beams or slanted walls are overtop. If there are, then adjust by using the Magnetic Home Red Polish. Add a dot on each corner with your intention of neutralizing the heavy energy.
✓ Doors open at night: Close them especially to a bathroom which can drain your energy.
✓ Clutter under the bed: Remove it creating clear space for energy to flow around your bed.

Mundane Solutions:
✓ Ask your doctor about a possible sleep study.
✓ Create a calm bedtime ritual that includes meditation, journaling your success and what you will do tomorrow.
✓ Wake up and go for a walk first thing, it resets your circadian rhythms.
✓ Wean yourself off caffeine opting for herbal teas instead.
✓ Make sure you have a good, supportive pillow that supports your cervical nerves properly through the night.

✓ If you wake up the same time each night, look up Chinese medicine wheels to see what that time might be telling you about your organs/health.

Affirmation: "I rest deeply and wake restored."

Challenge: I keep attracting the wrong romantic partner.

Ask yourself: Have I ever had a great romantic partner? If you knew what your block was, what would it be?

Possible Feng Shui Causes:
✓ Clutter in the Partnership area.
✓ Use of the color peach/apricot in the Partnership area or your bedroom. (Sparks passion, but can lead to infidelity.)
✓ Things representing unintentional singleness:
  • One nightstand (or two nightstands but one is significantly larger than the other)
  • Artwork portraying sadness, aggressiveness or singleness instead of happy couples or pairs of things.
  • Pairs of things are separated unintentionally. Example with a pair of chairs, one may be upstairs in a bedroom and the other used in a living room or a pair of candlesticks may be positioned apart, intentionally bring them together
  • No room for anyone to move in with you. Make space in your closet and bathroom for someone to come into your life and stay, even if it is 6" of closet space or clearing out a drawer.
  • Check your family of origin area if you suspect generational trauma. Make an adjustment with

the intention of healing ancestral wounds or your shadow self.

Mundane Solutions:

✓ Use the Values Checklist and discover what is most important to you. If you've been focused on attracting partners based on how they look, consider looking for someone with shared values instead.

✓ If you are an empath attracting narcissists (trust me, I know this all too well) the common denominator is you. Do the inner work. Find someone skilled in Shadow Work. Get to the bottom of why you don't even see the red flags or ignore the red flags when you do.

✓ Journal about past relationships, set clear boundaries, and focus on what you truly want.

Affirmation: "I attract someone who is kind and aligned with my values who reciprocates in giving and receiving love."

Challenge: I'm having problems with my daughter. We fight a lot.

Ask yourself: Is this natural growth and development for my daughter at this age? What am I not seeing about myself that might alleviate some of the tension?

Possible Feng Shui Causes:

✓ Bathrooms, stairways, clutter or missing pieces in the Children/Creativity area or the area represents your daughter:
  - The **oldest daughter** (or the only girl in the family) is represented in the Prosperity Area.
  - The **middle daughter** (you have three or more daughters, not the oldest and not the youngest) is represented in the (Fame & Reputation area).

- ○ The **youngest daughter** is represented in the Children/Creativity area. Adjust accordingly. Check the Children/Creativity area even if your daughter is not the youngest daughter.
- ✓ Bedrooms in equal/opposing command positions. You can hang a round-faceted crystal in between your two bedrooms to ease the tension. You could also place a round mirror on a wall closer to the front door, energetically moving her room out of the opposing command position. This makes her feel safer, like she doesn't have to be in charge of the situation and can fall back a bit. You could place a happy photo of the two of you in a visible area you both see frequently to remind you of the love you have for each other. Or use the photo as a cure wrapping red string around it 9 times and placing it in the appropriate life area either tucked in or taped in position.

Mundane Solutions:
- ✓ Take the Five Love Languages assessment together and make a concentrated effort to reflect your love for her in her language.
- ✓ Listen without judgment or sharing your stories trying to relate. Just listen.
- ✓ Let go of any attachment to the outcome.

Affirmation: "Our relationship is filled with love, understanding, and harmony."

Challenge: My career feels stuck.

Ask Yourself: Is there anything in my field that I really want to learn? If you could go a different direction, what would it be?

Possible Feng Shui Causes:

- ✓ Clutter, stagnant water or a blocked entry way in the Career area.
- ✓ The front door opens straight into a wall that feels too close blocking your vision, especially if the front entry way is in the Career Area.
- ✓ Every flat surface in your home has a tendency to be full. Move some of the items clearing energy for future things to happen.
- ✓ Your Fame and Reputation area needs some extra energy to support your career moving forward. Think of it as fire (Fame and Reputation) and water (Career) coming together to make steam!
- ✓ Your desk is facing a wall stopping you short. Move it to a command position with plenty of space to move forward.

Mundane Solutions:

- ✓ If you feel stuck in your income bracket, use Get Statements to activate your Reticular Cells and see opportunities you may have be missing.
- ✓ Update your résumé and work with a mentor.

Affirmation: "I receive new opportunities that expand my life's direction."

Challenge: My health keeps declining no matter what I do.

Ask Yourself: When did my health first start declining? Did something happen at that time?

Possible Feng Shui Causes:

- ✓ There is a bathroom, stairs, clutter or broken items in the center of the home. Repair them.

✓ You live on a Dead End. If there is a DEAD END sign, tie a red ribbon in a length of 9 around the signpost to neutralize the energy. Perform a sacred ceremony at the end of the road with the intention of moving the energy through.

✓ The home is situated on land with low chi. If plants and trees are not healthy, consider what may have happened to the land prior. Play healing solfeggio frequencies

✓ There are large electric lines or cell towers near the property.

Mundane Solutions:

✓ Schedule a health check-up.

✓ Do a liver cleanse and drink plenty of water with food and rest. Reset your energy.

✓ Consider a stem-cell patch.

✓ Do grounding by putting your bare feet on the earth to release negative ions.

Affirmation: "I am vibrant, healthy, and strong."

A STORY

Cell Towers & Power Lines are No Joke

I was called to consult on a home where my client had already placed a $20,000 earnest money check.

The road to the house was long, and as I drove, I kept noticing a large cell tower. It gave me an uneasy feeling. When I arrived at the property, I realized why – this massive tower was literally in the backyard, just beyond the fence.

The house itself carried eerie, heavy energy. As I walked through, I had the strong impression that something tragic had happened there – possibly a drowning in the pool or even a death inside the home. I advised my client not to move forward with the purchase.

Still, reluctant to part with such a large earnest money deposit, he consulted a high monk from his home country of Singapore. The monk wrote back and told him: if he bought the property, his life would be cut in half.

That was enough for him. He walked away from the deal.

Challenge: My children are not motivated or are struggling in school.

Ask Yourself: Besides being on a cell phone, watching television or playing video games, what is it that my children really love to do? What brings them joy?

Possible Feng Shui Causes:
- ✓ The Creativity/Children and Knowledge & Wisdom area are missing, cluttered or have neglected items.
- ✓ No proper workspace. Create an area in your Knowledge & Wisdom area or choose Creativity/Children area for special projects if possible. Metal is organizing so choose metal or white baskets if needed. Keep it simple and clear in a command position. You can add the color blue to the desk. Hang a round faceted crystal above the desk for good energy and clarity.

Mundane Solutions:
- ✓ Create structured homework time. Set a timer for 50 minutes. (That is about all we can absorb at one time. Maybe 30 minutes for younger children.) Then take a creative recharge and do something fun.
- ✓ Get curious if your children are kinesthetic, visual or auditory learners. Maybe they focus better when they

eat or drink something while they learn (water is always good, the brain needs hydration.)

✓ Encourage creative expression and celebrate achievements. Keep in mind that there are nine areas of genius. Not everyone is strong in reading, writing and arithmetic.

✓ Create a vision board and place it on their vision wall (first place they see in the morning) along with any academic awards.

Affirmation: "My children are inspired, motivated, and successful in their learning."

Challenge: I feel disconnected from my intuition.

Ask Yourself: When do you feel like you lost that connection? Were you young? Did it start with a new relationship? Or did something happen?

Possible Feng Shui Causes:

✓ Poor light, clutter, blocked pathways in the Knowledge & Wisdom area. Create a meditation garden if there is a missing piece or a meditation area/alter in this area.

✓ Bathroom, stairway or cluttered in the center of the home. Hang a round-faceted crystal with a red string in a length of 9 from the ceiling with an intention of clarity.

Mundane Solutions:

✓ Start by honoring the first thought that pops into your head before your monkey mind takes over.

✓ Learn what it feels like when you are right. Does it hit your stomach? Do you get goosebumps? Do you hear a voice?

✓ Take an intuition class.

✓ Write Angel Pages.

✓ Meditate.

Affirmation: "I trust my inner guidance and make clear decisions."

Challenge: I feel directionless in life.

Ask Yourself: Am I bored and playing too small? If I could wave a magic wand and be doing anything I would love to do without any concerns for money or what people think, what would I do?

Possible Feng Shui Causes:
- ✓ Clutter, stagnant water or a blocked entry way in the Career area. If there is a broken water feature here, fix it or replace it. Add a photo of you in a black frame when you were doing something with purpose that you loved.
- ✓ Bathroom, stairway or cluttered in the Center of the home. Hang a round-faceted crystal with a red string in a length of 9 from the ceiling with an intention of clarity.

Mundane Solutions:
- ✓ Take ten minutes and write quickly and without judgement or overthinking what you would like your life to look like 18 months from today. Include what you would like to do, be and have. It can be a story, bullet points, a combination. Set a time and write as quickly as you can and stop when the timer goes off.
- ✓ Hire a coach, someone who has done at least some of the things you want to do.
- ✓ Think of something so big that you could do that when you actually bring that idea to fruition you would feel alive and fulfilled.

Affirmation: "I move forward with clarity, purpose, and joy."

Challenge: I'm always there for others, but they don't support me when I need help.

Ask Yourself: Does helping others make me feel in control in some way? Do I end up feeling resentful and depleted of energy?

Possible Feng Shui Causes:

- ✓ **Clutter blocking energy, broken or unused items in Helpful People/Travel and Partnership areas.** Add a photo of your favorite deity (Jesus, angels, etc.) in the Helpful People/Travel area. See yourself receiving help in unexpected ways. Make sure your Partnership area is strengthened with pairs of things.
- ✓ Singleness messages throughout your home. Add pairs of things.

Mundane Solutions:

- ✓ For nine days shut off the giving spigot. When people ask you to do something, simply say *no*. Observe how you feel, maybe you feel guilty, maybe you miss the feeling of importance. Maybe you feel like you have more energy.
- ✓ If some people are taking advantage of you, reduce the time and energy you give to them or cut them off completely. Imagine a mirrored shield that their energy is reflected back to them.
- ✓ If we give from an empty cup, we feel drained and resentful. But when we fill ourselves first – like standing under a waterfall with our cup overflowing – giving feels effortless and joyful. Take care of yourself first, and let others receive from your overflow.

Affirmation: "I receive to overflowing."

Challenge: I'm stressed and overwhelmed.

Ask Yourself: What is the worst that could happen if I took a fifteen-minute timeout to do something I love?

Possible Feng Shui Causes:

- ✓ There is clutter everywhere or rooms have multiple purposes. Play a singing bowl or bell with the intention of the clutter being lighter and easier to organize. Then start decluttering a manageable space - a room, desktop or drawer. Define a purpose for the space and remove what doesn't belong energetically.
- ✓ Clutter on your desk, in your office or in your bedroom. Declutter these personal spaces. Use metal or white baskets for organization.
- ✓ Too much personal stuff lacking purpose. Choose one object that lifts your energy to provide a visual focal point when you walk into or through the room.

Mundane Solutions:

- ✓ This is an Abraham Hicks process: Take a lined piece of paper and draw a line straight down the middle. On the Top Right Side, write "The Manager.". Under this make a list of everything you want done. Now, on the Top Left Side write "Me." Go through the list on the right and choose three to five things you are going to do today - 100% for certain. The rest you turn over to The Manager. (You'll be amazed at what gets done on The Manager side without you doing it.)
- ✓ Rather than continually overwhelming yourself with a to-do list. Start writing down a success list. Write down the things you've completed and the successes you've had for the day. Review those the night before you go to bed.
- ✓ Rather than labeling yourself as a procrastinator, try seeing yourself as a **high-level prioritizer**. When I was raising three active teenagers while running my

business, it often felt like I was juggling a hundred balls in the air. Things didn't always get done early, and I used to beat myself up for procrastinating. Then one day it clicked: *I'm not procrastinating – I'm prioritizing.* I may not do everything weeks or even days in advance, but I rarely, if ever, miss a deadline.

✓ Take a meditation class.

Affirmation: "I am calm, centered and peaceful."

Challenge: I'm newly divorced and now I feel like I have to start all over with a new job, new home and new life.

Ask yourself: How can I make the most of this blessing of being given a fresh start in my life?

Possible Feng Shui Causes:

Well, with this kind of fresh start we don't have to look at what has happened. Let's focus your energy on New Beginnings in the Family of Origin area and The Future in Children & Creativity where you can develop your confidence about your future.

✓ The Family of Origin area is the space of roots, vitality, and fresh starts. It represents both the support of your ancestry and the energy of new beginnings sprouting forward. When this area is strong, you feel stable, supported, and ready to grow into new opportunities. Its energy is fueled by the Wood element – think tall trees, fresh shoots, and endless possibilities.. Stagnant energy blocks fresh growth.

  o Clear out clutter, especially forgotten boxes or old belongings, and invite in fresh air and light.

  o Fireplaces or too many fire elements (red, triangles) burn up the wood energy of Family of Origin. Place a healthy green plant nearby, add

119

a water feature or black accents to temper the fire.

- ○ Dead or Dying Plants: Wood is about vitality – so struggling plants symbolize blocked or failing new beginnings. Replace with thriving greenery, bamboo, or a money tree to reinforce renewal.
- ○ Missing or Cut-Off Corners weaken support and makes it harder to create a fresh start. Use mirrors, lights, or landscaping outdoors to symbolically call in the missing energy.

Mundane Solutions

- ✓ Hire a solid life coach. Now more than ever you need someone to energetically align with you and hold the space for you to take on this journey with confidence and grace.
- ✓ Find healthy ways to meet new people. Join a church, networking groups, go to meetups or take a class that interests you.
- ✓ Create a vision board of what you want to have happen within the next 18 months and hang it where you will see it often.
- ✓ Be gentle with yourself. Change is difficult no matter how you slice it. Long hot showers and baths help to release energy and integrate the new energy. Do things that you love: get a massage, take a painting class, schedule regular massages or invite a friend over to have dinner and watch a good inspirational movie about a great comeback.

Affirmation: "I am supported, rooted, and ready for fresh new beginnings to flow into my life. I see my future unfolding beautifully."

Challenge: I struggle to maintain healthy habits.

Ask yourself: Am I defining my own set of healthy habits or am I adopting other's idea of healthy habits that don't feel good to me or work with my lifestyle? What is my greatest challenge? Time? Discipline? Motivation? Self-worth? Doing too much for others and not giving myself enough attention?

Possible Feng Shui Causes:
- ✓ Too much clutter in the Health area. Clear the area and do an energetic cleanse signifying your own healthy cleanse. You can smudge with sage, spray with salt water or holy water, use a singing bowl or bell. See yourself cleansing (especially your liver) and renewing. Call in the sparkles.
- ✓ The Kitchen Area: The kitchen represents nourishment. A messy fridge, old pantry items, or poor lighting can block the flow of healthy habits.
- ✓ The Dining Area: The dining room also represents health and vitality. Make sure you are eating where you feel fully supported and not visible from the front door.
- ✓ The Bedroom: Review your bedroom and make sure that it is a supportive sanctuary.

Mundane Solutions:
- ✓ Start your day with a brisk walk before 9:00 am. This resets your circadian rhythms. Fifteen minutes helps a lot.
- ✓ Take on one new healthy habit. Rather than doing everything at once, start with one new thing. Maybe add more vegetables to your diet, go for a morning walk, drink more water, give up diet soda, a weekly yoga class, weekly massage, etc.
- ✓ Create a vision board of a new, healthier you.
- ✓ Only buy healthy food and find simple recipes for cooking.

✓ Be more active. Take the stairs, walk, ride an eBike. Do things you enjoy. Make it fun.

Affirmation: "I joyfully choose habits that energize and nourish me. My home and body are aligned with health, vitality, and flow."

Chapter 11

Mental & Emotional Wellbeing

We live in a world where screens compete for our attention almost every waking hour. Notifications, endless scrolling, and too many hours indoors have quietly taken a toll. Add to this the pressures of modern life – deadlines, bills, family responsibilities – and it's no wonder stress and anxiety have become everyday companions.

Science is now confirming what many of us already feel in our bodies: stress changes the brain. A recent study showed that the more we visualize things going wrong, the more the hypothalamus – the part of the brain that regulates stress responses – actually grows. This enlargement fuels greater anxiety, creating a cycle of "expecting the worst." The good news? The opposite is also true. Practices that calm the nervous system can shrink the hypothalamus, bringing balance back to the body and mind.

Manifesting Feng Shui gives us a powerful, practical way to support this inner balance through our outer environment. When your space reflects harmony, it naturally helps calm your mind, settle your emotions, and support clarity.

On your Magnetic Game Board, several areas are especially powerful for mental and emotional health. Here's how to work with them:

Health (Your Center)

The very heart of your home reflects your own center. When this space feels clear, light, and open, it supports harmony in your body and mind. But when the center is cluttered, blocked, or heavy, it often shows up as mental fog, emotional instability, or just a sense of being "off."

What you can do:

- ✓ Clear away clutter or heavy objects from the middle of your home.
- ✓ Bring in bright light, a round crystal, or fresh flowers to lift the energy.
- ✓ Spend a few quiet minutes standing in the center, hand over your heart, and imagine your whole being settling into balance.

Knowledge & Wisdom

This area is your sanctuary for reflection, learning, and peace of mind. When it's strong, your thoughts quiet down, your intuition sharpens, and you feel more resilient. When it's neglected, you might notice anxious thought loops, overthinking, or feeling disconnected from your own wisdom.

What you can do:

- ✓ Create a cozy meditation nook, reading chair, or a simple altar here.
- ✓ Add symbols of wisdom – books, candles, spiritual art, or calming colors like deep blues or soft greens.
- ✓ Use this space daily, even if just for five minutes of mindful breathing.

Family of Origin

This area is tied to your roots – your ancestry, your emotional foundation, and your vitality. When it's in harmony, you feel supported, flexible, and strong. When it's out of balance, you may notice old family stress, conflicts, or a feeling of being drained.

What you can do:

- ✓ Place healthy, thriving plants here to represent growth and resilience.
- ✓ Honor your roots with photos, heirlooms, or symbols that bring you strength (but avoid anything that carries painful memories).
- ✓ Add a splash of green, wood elements, or even a piece of art that reminds you of renewal and vitality.

When you strengthen these areas on your Magnetic Game Board, you're not just decorating - you're gently reprogram-ming your nervous system. Your home begins to hold you in balance, reminding you daily that peace, resilience, and clarity are always available to you.

Everyday Practices to Ease Anxiety

Balancing your environment is powerful and pairing it with mindful daily habits makes the results even stronger. Small actions can interrupt cycles of stress and give your body and mind a chance to reset.

- ✓ **Take three slow, deep breaths** whenever you feel anxious. It immediately shifts your nervous system into a calmer state.
- ✓ **Meditation or quiet reflection** strengthens your inner wisdom and shrinks the stress center in the brain.
- ✓ **Spend time in nature** – better yet, barefoot. Walking on grass, soil, or sand grounds your body and releases tension.
- ✓ **Yoga or gentle stretching** restores flow to the body and mind, releasing stuck emotions.
- ✓ **A brisk morning walk** helps recalibrate circadian rhythms, boosts energy, and sets a positive tone for the rest of your day.
- ✓ **Unplug from screens regularly** to reduce mental clutter and overstimulation. Even fifteen minutes of stillness without a device makes a difference.
- ✓ **Bring in calming natural elements** – a plant, a water fountain, or natural light – so your home itself reminds your body to relax.

Your home is more than just a container for your life – it's a reflection of your inner state. By clearing and balancing key areas in your home, and by practicing simple daily rituals that nurture calm, you create an environment that supports your mental and emotional wellbeing. Instead of adding to the noise, your space becomes your sanctuary: a steadying force in a world that often feels chaotic.

Chapter 12

Energy Check!

Listen, if you've got repairs in your home that you're ignoring because they "cost too much," then here's the truth bomb: that energy of "too expensive" or "I don't have enough" is echoing through your house like a bad karaoke song. And guess what? With the Law of Attraction, whatever you focus on, you amplify. So, if you keep vibing with "I can't afford this," the universe will keep handing you situations to prove yourself right. Ouch.

Now, do I expect you to remodel your whole house overnight? No. I don't even expect you to do any remodeling because that is not what Magnetic Home is about. But I do expect you to do what you can. Tighten the loose doorknob, replace the burnt-out bulb, patch the wall, fix the wobbly chair. These little acts tell your home – and your subconscious – that you're moving from lack into the flow of prosperity in all Nine Life Areas.

One of my favorite affirmations (and it works like magic) is this one that came to me a few years ago:

"I have more than enough time, money, and energy to do what I want, when I want."

It's short, it's sassy, and it gets straight to the point. Whenever I catch myself thinking something is too expensive or too much work, I stop, breathe, and repeat that line until it drowns out the old story.

Start where you are, use what you have, and shift what you can. If all you can do today is clear a drawer or finally glue that broken handle back on, do it. Every little shift sends a message to the universe: *I'm ready for more. I'm taking care of my space, so take care of me.*

And above all – have fun with it. Your home should feel like a partner in manifesting your dreams, not a list of chores dragging you down. So, lighten up, make the changes you can, and let go of the stress. Your house – and your life – will thank you.

Fix & Repair

- ☐ Repair or replace anything broken (doors, drawers, handles, appliances). Visualize a healthy and happy home as a reflection of a healthy and happy you!
- ☐ Replace burned-out lightbulbs. Use bright white or soft white depending on your preference.
- ☐ Fix squeaky hinges, leaky faucets, running toilets. YouTube is a great resource!
- ☐ Patch holes, cracks, or chipped paint/walls. When you paint, you can add a drop of red fingernail polish while speaking your intention to enhance the energy of the paint. Hold the intention for the space while you paint. This really shifts the energy quickly. Also, choose paint colors that are clear and not muddy.

Clear & Clean

- ☐ Declutter the entryway (let energy flow in easily).
- ☐ Clear surfaces of excess "stuff." Your desktop/countertops reflect your vision in life, your future.
- ☐ Dust corners and behind furniture (where stagnant energy hides). If you feel a spot with dark energy, you

can clap or ring a bell to get the energy unstuck and moving!

☐ Wash windows. Windows represent your vision and also the children of the home. When you wash your windows, think about being clear as you are moving forward in life.

☐ Vacuum/mop regularly to refresh energy.

Energize & Uplift

Think about being a little ray of sunshine as you dance around your home making it sparkle and shine with these adjustments.

☐ Open windows for fresh air. Breathe deeply and use your hands to wave in the fresh air cleansing your space with renewed energy.

☐ Add healthy, thriving plants (remove any dead/dying ones). If you don't have a green thumb or limited sunlight in a room, fake plants work, too. Studies have shown that seeing plants (real or fake) can uplift mood. However, there are greater health benefits with real plants.

☐ Bring in fresh flowers or natural elements (wood, stone, water). Remember to remove flowers when they are wilted. You can say a blessing when you do.

☐ Use essential oils, incense, or sage to uplift and clear energy.

☐ Use clapping or a nice sounding bell to uplift and clear energy.

☐ Adjust lighting so no area is too dark or harshly lit.

Align & Intend

☐ Check your front door: clean, working, welcoming. When I traveled to some of the poorest of the poor places with dirt floors, I would see women sweeping the front of their home to clear leaves and debris. It was a morning ritual. Whatever you do, do it with intention.

☐ Place a doormat that feels inviting. Make sure it is wider than your doorway.

☐ Arrange furniture so energy flows easily and you feel comfortable where you spend the majority of your time. There is a lot on this in the feng shui section.

☐ Add meaningful artwork or décor that inspires you and makes you feel good.

Chapter 13

Windows:

Portals of Energy, Vision, and Opportunity

In feng shui, windows are the eyes of your home. They are portals of chi – the vital life-force energy – connecting your inner world with the vast, expansive world outside. Just as your personal vision shapes the life you create, your windows shape the energy that flows into your space. Where walls ground and protect you, windows invite movement, clarity, and new opportunities.

Why What You See Matters

The view from your windows reflects your vision for life. Every glance outward is a reminder of what you are focusing on, whether consciously or not. A beautiful garden, tree-lined street, or open sky nourishes your vision with creativity, calm, and inspiration. In contrast, cluttered lots, broken fences, or busy highways may cloud your outlook, signaling distraction or limitation.

Your environment mirrors your inner state. So, the quality of your view isn't just about scenery – it's about how clearly you see your path ahead.

✓ **Positive Views**: Trees, gardens, water, mountains, or wide skies strengthen your vision of abundance, vitality, and clarity.

✓ **Negative Views**: Dead-end alleys, neglected properties, or stagnant spaces may quietly dim your vision, stirring fatigue or frustration.

reflect

What do you notice when you look out your windows? Which is your favorite? How does it make you feel? What changes would you make? What about your least favorite window?

If your view is less than inviting (or lacks expansion) consider how you could make your view more beautiful. Can you build a fence with a beautiful trumpet vine? Or plant a flowering tree that draws the eye beyond neighboring clutter?

Tending to your windows and view with care, you align your outer environment with the inner picture of the life you are manifesting.

✓ **Keep them sparkling**: Clean windows support clear vision and fresh perspective.

✓ **Frame your view**: Curtains or treatments can guide your focus toward beauty, reminding you of your desired reality

✓ **Add activators**: Plants, crystals, or wind chimes bring vibrancy and joy into your field of vision.

✓ **Use mirrors mindfully**: Let them reflect beauty, amplifying a positive outlook and expansive possibilities.

The Subtle Power of Orientation

Each window direction influences both the energy in your home and the vision you hold for your life:

- **East-facing** windows: New beginnings, vitality, and fresh perspectives.
- **South-facing** windows: Recognition, inspiration, and visibility – seeing yourself in your power.
- **West-facing** windows: Creativity, joy, and playful visioning.
- **North-facing** windows: Wisdom, career flow, and guidance from mentors – helping you see your path clearly.

When you align your windows with intention, you're not only inviting chi into your home – you're strengthening your personal vision. Each view becomes a living reminder that what you choose to see is what you invite into your life.

Chapter 14

Is it Time to Declutter?

Your stuff is not neutral. It either lifts you up or drags you down – and it can take a surprising amount of energy to manage it all or hardly any if what you own brings you copious amounts of joy.

Everything you own, owns you right back.

I learned this lesson early in my career. About twenty years ago, I consulted with a childless, older couple who were downsizing from city life and retiring to a farm. When I told them, *"what you own, owns you,"* they nodded like they understood. But when moving day came, they hired a truck to haul 35,000 pounds of books and belongings. Yes, you read that right – 35,000 pounds. They even built a huge shed on their new property just to house their "stuff."

Fast forward to now: they live in a two-room assisted living facility. Frieda, the wife, laughed as she reminded me of my words. The things in that shed? Never organized. Never used. And eventually, a massive burden when it was time to move again and start giving things away.

That's the thing: clutter doesn't just eat up your space – it eats up your life force energy. Every drawer, every pile, every box of "someday" items tugs on you, whether you realize it or not.

A STORY

A Glamour Goddess Needs Her Clothes

My friend Georgia is a true Glamour Goddess. She adores clothing, jewelry, boots, and scarves – and she wears them with a radiant confidence that is magnetic. What's so inspiring about Georgia is how she brings this passion into her home. Even her guest bedroom holds the most charming bedroom set from her grade school days, carrying a sense of history and delight.

And here's what I admire most: Georgia intentionally creates the ultimate Magnetic Home. Every corner is filled with things she loves. Whenever she moves to a new house, she makes sure there's a plan for expanding her closet – whether it means converting an attic, a garage, or an extra bedroom.

Her wardrobe is meticulously organized, not out of obligation, but out of devotion to what brings her joy. She has even designed her own display fixtures so that her bracelets, necklaces, and earrings are all visible and easy to reach. Her accessories shine like little treasures on display and stepping into her space feels like walking into her personal sanctuary of a modern-day boutique.

This girl struts her stuff, laughing all the way. Her husband honors her for the fashionista she is! What a pair!

Georgia's example is a beautiful reminder that a Magnetic Home doesn't have to look like anyone else's. It simply has to reflect what lights you up. For Georgia, it's glamour. For you, it might be books, art, plants, or travel mementos. Whatever it is, fill your home with what you love, and watch how it elevates not only your space, but your entire life.

Choose What to Let Go and What to Keep with a Clear Vision and Intention

Every home tells a story, and the choices you make about what you keep, display, and organize shape that story. Some of us love efficiency and using what we already have, sourcing treasures from thrift stores, garage sales, or repurposing items. For example, in my own home, I keep what I use most for cooking and eating in a small cupboard by the sink. My jars of nuts, peanut butter, and honey (all with matching lids and clearly labeled) are stored on a repurposed wine rack, ready for breakfast each morning. Simple and easy.

My clothing is mostly basic neutrals, with a few pops of color. Malas and scarves from my travels are displayed where I can enjoy them. Items my kids use when they visit for holidays are kept in one organized cupboard. I travel frequently for one- to two-month stretches, so each home base contains exactly what I need for that season and location.

I'm also designing my 1870 cabin on five acres in Missouri to be a sanctuary for single women who want to relax, create, and restore. Every detail – from the recipe book and sourdough starter to the cozy sleeping arrangements – is designed to support a single person's experience, or a girl's weekend experience for two or three soul sisters. The point is this: we all have unique needs and styles. Before you hold onto things – or let go – picture the home you truly want to create. How do you want to *feel* when you're in it?

Flip through magazines, scroll Pinterest, or simply daydream about your ideal space. Without intention, it's easy to accumulate things that weigh you down or to release items you may actually want. Trust that if you need something later, the Universe (or your resourcefulness) will support you.

Clarity & Intention

Your home is a reflection of your energy. To align your space with your life, take a moment to check in with yourself:

- What feelings or experiences do I want my home to support?
- How does each room currently make me feel – joyful, stressed, relaxed?
- What intentions do I want to set for my bedroom, living area, kitchen, and workspace?
- Which areas feel most alive, and which feel stagnant? Why?
- If my home could speak, what would it tell me about my current energy?

Letting Go

Letting go is just as important as bringing in what you love. Items that no longer serve your vision for a Magnetic Home can quietly drain your energy. If you have something that you aren't sure about letting go, ask yourself:

- Does this support my ideal home and lifestyle?
- Does this carry positive memories or emotions or am I ready to let it go?
- How does seeing this affect my mood or energy?
- If I removed this today, how might my space – and my life – shift?
- Does this bring me pure joy and feel fully aligned with my soul?

Living the Magnetic Lifestyle

A Magnetic Home isn't a one-time project, it's a lifestyle. Consider how your day-to-day habits can support your intentions:

- How can I maintain a home that consistently supports my energy and intentions?
- Which daily or weekly practices keep my home aligned and vibrant?
- What small adjustments could instantly lift the energy of a room?
- How does my home make me feel when I walk through the front door?
- How do I want visitors to feel when they enter my home?

Notes

Notes

Notes

Chapter 15

Space Clearing:

Clearing Clutter, Clearing Energy

Space clearing is one of the most powerful tools to shift energy in your home. Every object, every corner, and even the air itself carries vibration. When energy stagnates, it can weigh on us in subtle but profound ways. Over the years, I've performed countless clearings and learned to "see" energy as it moves through a space.

I often notice it coming out of paintings or hiding in corners where energy has stagnated. One client had an entire bookshelf dedicated to self-help books. As I moved through the room, I could feel heavy, dark energy emanating from the shelf. It made perfect sense: authors share their trauma in these books. When we read them, we absorb that energy. And when we store them in our homes, it reinforces a message that we "need help," which can, in turn, attract more challenges.

Reading to grow and improve yourself is wonderful – but I encourage passing the book along once you've absorbed what you need. Don't let the energy of someone else's struggle accumulate in your home or linger on your nightstand.

Removing Stagnant Energy

Space clearing isn't just about objects; it's also about energy flow. I remember one morning I was completely overwhelmed. My home was in chaos – two toddlers had turned it into a whirlwind of toys, laundry, and dishes. To make matters more pressing, I was hosting a group of women that evening.

I knew that taking just 30 minutes to clear the energy would make the biggest difference. I opened the windows, grabbed my sacred Balinese bell, and began at the front door, moving around the perimeter of my home. Using the resonance of the bell, I started to pick up and release stagnant energy.

When I reached the master closet, something extraordinary happened. My body began to undulate, as though I were calling in the great gods. A guttural chant emerged from my solar plexus – completely unknown to me. Out of the corner of my eye, I saw three heavy boxes that had been sitting there for over a year start to sparkle holographically. I couldn't move them, they weren't mine, they belonged to my husband.

A few minutes later, I finished the clearing at the front door, and my husband walked in. I hid the bell behind my back, embarrassed he might have heard the chant. He asked what I was doing. I said, "Nothing." When I asked him why he was home in the middle of the workday, he said he felt an urge to help clean – he knew I was overwhelmed. I let him move freely while I continued clearing the space.

When I returned to the closet, my jaw dropped – the boxes were gone. I had no idea if they moved themselves or if he had done it. I asked him. "Did you move those boxes?"

He said, "Duh, who else would have moved them?" And just as quickly as he arrived, he left.

By the time my guests arrived that evening, the house was immaculate. Everything was in its place, except for a small stack of papers for me to review. I felt incredible – light, free, and ready to receive.

Lessons from Space Clearing

- ✓ **Energy Moves:** Space clearing brings stagnant energy into motion. Objects, corners, and rooms can shift in ways that surprise us.
- ✓ **Intent Matters:** Your intention sets the vibration. Even if no one else sees what you're doing, your energy creates profound change.
- ✓ **Clutter is Energy:** Old, unneeded, or misaligned items hold energy that can weigh you down. Let go, pass it on, or move it out.
- ✓ **Collaboration Happens:** Sometimes, clearing energy invites unseen assistance – from guides, angels, or simply inspiring others to help.
- ✓ **You Feel the Shift:** The most tangible sign of a successful clearing isn't just a clean space – it's the lightness you feel inside.

Space clearing teaches us that energy is alive. Every object, every corner, every room has a vibration that can support – or hinder – our lives. When we open ourselves to it, our homes speak to us in subtle ways, guiding us toward alignment, clarity, and joy.

Sometimes, these messages are quiet – a gentle nudge to release a book, rearrange a chair, or clear a corner. Other times, the energy is palpable, almost alive, revealing its own personality and history.

I experienced this firsthand in Thailand. I was dining at a small restaurant when my eyes landed on a three-foot-tall candle holder made from what appeared to be an antique carved musical instrument. The curves and details were exquisite, and three small shelves held tealight candles perfectly. I wanted to create something similar for a co-living resort I am developing south of Cancun.

As I took a photo, I noticed something extraordinary – not a glare on the lens, but the spirit of a dragon residing within the piece. The energy was palpable. Imagine the intention poured into carving that wood centuries ago, the music that once resonated through it, and now the joy of discovering and repurposing it. The dragon spirit was living proof that objects hold the stories, energy, and intention of their makers – and that our awareness can awaken that magic once more.

Chapter 16

The Spirit of All Things

There is a spirit to all things. We are not walking this journey alone. Each of us has benevolent angels and guides, gently nudging us toward our soul's highest path. When we open our hearts and quiet our minds, we can feel their presence, guiding us in subtle and profound ways.

This is true not only of people but also of our homes. Houses have a spirit, as do our belongings. They hold memories, energy, and a voice all their own. If we slow down enough to listen, our homes will speak to us. Sometimes it's a whisper: move this chair here, let this object go. Other times it's a deep knowing that a change is needed to better support our growth.

When we honor this conversation with our space, we begin to live in harmony with both the seen and unseen. Our homes can guide us in the outer journey just as our guides and angels support our inner path – offering clarity, support, and alignment every step of the way.

The Spirit in Every Object

Every item in your home carries energy. Some rooms feel heavy, stagnant, and draining. Others feel alive, fresh, and welcoming. That is the living vibration of all things at play.

A plant doesn't just decorate a corner; it breathes life into your home. A crystal doesn't just sparkle; it radiates subtle frequencies that can bring clarity and calm. Even simple items – a mug you love or a blanket you curl up in – hold the essence of comfort, love, and joy.

In a Magnetic Home, you choose consciously which spirits you allow to surround you. Clearing clutter isn't just tidying, its releasing stuck energy, old stories, and forgotten dreams. Bringing in objects that hold beauty, meaning, and vitality invites supportive spirits into your daily life. These things connect you with you on a soul level. A chipped dish can irritate you more than you realize, or a piece of artwork can bring tears of joy. You are not separate from your environment – you are in relationship with it. Like any relationship, it thrives when honored, respected, and infused with love and appreciation.

When you awaken to the spirit in all things, your home becomes a sacred partner. Every room hums with intention. Every corner becomes a prayer. Your home, infused with spirit, attracts the love, opportunities, and abundance your soul longs to experience in the here and now.

Awakening the Spirit of Your Home

You can connect with the spirit of your home through a simple blessing ritual. No special tools are required – just your presence, breath, and intention.

Step 1: Prepare the Space

✓ Open windows to allow fresh air to flow.
✓ Light a candle or burn incense for illumination and purification.
✓ Place a bowl of water or a small plant nearby to invite life.

Step 2: Center Yourself

✓ Stand in the middle of your home or room.
✓ Take three deep breaths, grounding in the present moment.

✓ Place your hand over your heart and silently thank your home for sheltering and supporting you.

Step 3: Call in the Spirit of Your Home

✓ Walk slowly through each room.
✓ Gently touch objects, furniture, or walls and say: "I honor the spirit within you. Thank you for supporting my life."
✓ Notice any feelings that arise. You may feel called to release some items or rearrange others – this is your intuition guiding you.

Step 4: Seal the Intention

✓ Return to the center of your home.
✓ Speak a blessing aloud: "May this home be filled with light, love, and harmony. May every object and corner reflect the highest vibration of peace, abundance, and joy."
✓ Imagine the entire space glowing with golden light, alive and smiling back at you.

A STORY

The Sparkles

I learned about the spirit of all things academically in training, but the first time I truly experienced it was in a Minneapolis penthouse. My client, David, had a home impeccably furnished – matching curved, cream-colored sofas, a display case of expensive objects, perfectly curated lighting. Everything was beautiful... yet it looked and felt lifeless.

As we began the consultation, I asked David what he wanted to create or change. As you now know, intention is always the key – it shifts energy effortlessly. Then, we started to walk in each life area to see what was aligning with his intention and what seemed out of alignment. In the guest bathroom, newly updated with green floral wallpaper and gold fixtures, I heard a whisper: *"Yes, I'm beautiful, but no one has ever been here to enjoy me."* I thought I imagined it, so I moved on to his closet.

On one side: dark business suits, energy dull and heavy. Across: Hawaiian shirts in every color, sparkling holographically with joy. His clothes were telling me what his heart already knew: he hated his work but stayed out of obligation to his family. His personal clothing sparkled with freedom, fun, and joy.

In the kitchen and dining area, the chairs spoke to me: *"We are beautiful, but no one has ever sat on us. We want to be loved and appreciated."* By now, I couldn't ignore the conversation this beautiful apartment and its furnishings where having with me, I nervously told David what the dining room chairs were saying. Instead of thinking me crazy, he agreed, acknowledging that no one had been invited to his home since he moved in three years prior. I was the first.

Here is a profound truth: beauty alone does not create life-force energy. It is connecting with what brings us joy and meaning – honoring the spirit of our spaces – that makes a home come alive.

Even the most carefully curated homes can feel dead if the energy is stagnant or the owner is constantly unhappy. When we are willing to listen, respond, and dance with the energy of our belongings, magic unfolds. Our homes become allies, supporting our growth, abundance, and joy. It is up to us to add our energy with mindful intention.

It all starts with what we want – and the willingness to create a living relationship with our space. This isn't normal – but it is magical.

Chapter 17

Magnetizing Your Home Office

Your office is the command center of your life's work. It's where your vision takes form, where ideas spark, and where opportunities find you. Placing your office near the front of your home is ideal, it symbolically opens the door for clients, resources, and energy to flow in with ease.

Even if you never see clients at home, this placement matters. We are always considering the energy. If your clients had to walk through your home to get to your office, you would not like that. Neither does energy. Moving your office to the front of the home, makes your work feel visible, supported, and accessible. This is a space for connection and business. Positioning your office near the front naturally creates a flow of abundance.

Think of your office as your stage, your launchpad, your magnet for success. When you set it up with intention, it not only supports productivity – it amplifies your purpose and who you are in the world.

The Command Position: Where Your Desk Belongs

Your desk is the most important piece in your office. It represents your career, your contribution to the world, and the flow of opportunities that come to you. Its placement directly influences how you feel about your work and how others perceive you. It also helps you to focus on the tasks at hand.

Ideally, your desk should be in **command position**:

✓ You can clearly see the door without being directly in line with it.
✓ Your back is against a solid wall (not a window).
✓ You have a clear view of the room, allowing you to feel secure, empowered, and in charge.

When your desk is pushed against a wall or your back faces the door, you may feel unsupported or creatively blocked. If this can't be changed, remedies include: placing a mirror to reflect the door, hanging inspiring artwork to create a sense of vision, or adding tall-backed chairs and plants for symbolic support.

Remember: the way you sit at your desk reflects how you face the world.

Creating Support and Flow

✓ **Your chair matters**: Choose one that is strong and supportive. Place it against a wall if possible – symbolic "backing" for your career.
✓ **Your desk size matters: It** represents your vision. If it is too small and cramped, it keeps you small. If it is too large, you might feel overwhelmed. Choose a desk that gives you enough space and vision to stay organized. A cluttered desk scatters your thoughts, while a clear one opens space for clarity and flow. A writing desk can be smaller to keep you focused, while running a large company with many projects requires a bigger work surface. Keep only what supports your current projects on top. This goes for your computer as well. Be mindful of all the windows open and the distractions they bring. Keep only the files you need open and you will find it easier to focus.

✓ **Arrange with intention**: Place plants or flowers to your left (Prosperity area) for growth, your phone or computer to the right for communication (Helpful People area), and a lamp or crystal near you for clarity and inspiration. I like to hang a round-faceted crystal above where I sit for clarity and organization.

✓ **Light fuels creativity**: Natural light is best, but warm lamps or full-spectrum bulbs keep your energy lifted.

✓ **Create a vision wall.** This is the wall that you see most. It's a great place for an inspirational vision board, photos of awards you've received, a project completion board, or whatever inspires you most.

✓ **Surround yourself with symbols that uplift**: Artwork, meaningful objects, or reminders of your goals. Let your office reflect your *vision*, not your stress. Avoid using your office to double as a storage room. Your workspace should feel purposeful, not heavy.

Activating the Four Areas for Business Success

These four areas of your office, home and desk are especially powerful for manifesting abundance and opportunity:

✓ **Prosperity**: Place lush plants, citrine or jade, or symbols of financial growth. You can also use the color black (water) and the color purple.

✓ **Fame & Reputation**: This is how the world sees you. Display awards, branding, or light a red candle to amplify recognition. Pyramids are great, too.

✓ **Career** Keep this pathway open and uncluttered. Add water elements or affirmations that declare your path is clear.

✓ **Helpful People/Travel**: Place images of mentors, angels, travel, or collaborations you'd like to attract.

Keep space open for new connections. This invites synchronicities in. You think about it and it appears.

When these zones are activated, your business becomes easier. You produce greater results with less physical energy on your part. You tap into the Universal flow.

Giving Yourself the Space to Create

A friend once told me about her new office job. Her desk was pushed against a wall with her back to the door. "It gives me room to spread out samples," she explained.

But when I asked how it felt, she admitted: "It's boring. I don't feel productive. Honestly, it's like I can't see past this wall."

Her words revealed what we know: when you face a wall, you limit your vision. With your back to the door, you feel unsupported. Over time, this drains your energy and stifles creativity because not "feeling right" takes up too much energy to be creative and in the flow.

Your environment always mirrors your inner life. If your office feels blocked, so will your ideas. If it feels open, supported, and alive – you'll feel that too.

Ritual for Calling in Clients

If you're ready to welcome more opportunities, try this beautiful ritual:

1. Gather nine cups of bird seed, rice, or grass seed.
2. Hold it in your hands and bless it with your intention – to feed the unseen, honor spirit, and invite clients or opportunities.
3. Starting at your front door, sprinkle the seed as you walk toward the nearest main road.
4. Circle back, continuing to sprinkle as you return home.

This ritual nourishes what is hungry, clears stagnant energy, and symbolically opens pathways for new clients, connections, and abundance to flow directly to you.

A STORY

My Own Office Practice

As an entrepreneur providing for my family for over twenty years, I always made my office a top priority (along with my bedroom, kitchen, and dining spaces). I often used the architecturally designed dining room as my office – right near the front of the house.

I made sure my back was to a wall and that I had a strong, supportive chair. The wall in front of me became my *vision wall*. Sometimes I hung a whiteboard with affirmations. Other times, I placed a vision board or images of potential business projects. These kept me focused – consciously and subconsciously – on what mattered most to my family's prosperity.

Every year around my birthday, I updated my vision board. I used a framed piece of art I'd found at a garage sale – it looked beautiful and intentional, not like scraps of cardboard. Sometimes I hung it at the foot of my bed, so I saw it morning and night. Other times it lived in my closet, so it was the first thing I saw walking in and out.

I've also tucked inspiring cutouts around my home – like a photo of a strong, toned woman walking, which I kept by my bathroom mirror. I've even written affirmations on mirrors with a dry-erase marker. All of these little "vision walls" reminded me daily of the future I was creating.

It's like driving a car. If you've ever driven long distances, you know the experience of "waking up" and realizing you don't remember the last few miles. Part of your mind was steering, while the other part was off envisioning something else. That windshield time opens portals to higher consciousness.

That's what vision boards do: they shift your reticular activating system (RAS), training your mind to notice opportunities that match your vision.

The Reticular Activating System: Training Your Mind to See

Your brain has a built-in filter called the Reticular Activating System (RAS). It decides what information gets your attention and what gets filtered out. With billions of bits of data coming at you every second, the RAS chooses only a fraction for your conscious mind to notice.

Here's the key: your RAS prioritizes whatever you tell it is important. If you've ever bought a new car and suddenly see that same model everywhere, that's your RAS at work. The car was always there, but your brain now recognizes it as relevant.

Vision boards and vision walls work in the same way. By surrounding yourself with images, words, and symbols of what you desire, you are literally programming your RAS to seek them out in the world. It's not just wishful thinking – it's a neurological process of directing attention.

Vision Boards and Vision Walls

A vision board is a curated collection of images and affirmations representing the life you want to create. A vision wall expands that concept, making the entire wall in front of you a canvas for your future. Whether it's a whiteboard with affirmations, framed artwork layered with images, or even magazine cutouts taped where you'll see them daily, the key is repetition. Every glance becomes a subtle reminder to your subconscious: *This is what I'm moving toward. This is what matters.*

Connecting to Higher Consciousness

While the RAS works on the neurological level, visioning also activates something deeper. The more often you see and feel your vision, the more you align with a higher field of consciousness – the place where inspiration, synchronicity, and guidance live.

This is where the practical and the mystical merge. Your RAS primes your mind to notice opportunities you might otherwise overlook. At the same time, your consistent focus raises your vibration and connects you to higher guidance. You begin to experience "coincidences" that are anything but. The right people call. Unexpected opportunities appear. Ideas drop in while you're driving or showering.

Your vision boards and walls act like antennas, broadcasting your intention outward while tuning your inner frequency. They help bridge the physical mind with the unseen field of possibility.

Your office is more than a workspace. It's the vision-holder for your future. When it's set up with intention, it doesn't just support your business – it magnetizes opportunities, connections, and success into your life.

Chapter 18

Making Room for Love

Love is one of the greatest desires of the human heart. Whether you are calling in a soulmate, deepening a marriage, or opening to greater self-love, your home can become a powerful ally. Our outer environment mirrors our inner world. If your space is cluttered, imbalanced, or filled only with reminders of the past, it may be sending the message: *there's no room for love here.*

By shifting your physical environment, you open the energetic doorway for love to arrive. Each change becomes a declaration: *I am ready. Love is welcome in my life.*

Step One: Release the Past

Before new love can enter fully, old energy must be released. Holding onto items from past relationships – photos, gifts, love letters, or furniture – keeps you tied to what has already ended.

Create a ritual of release:
- ✓ Gather items connected to old loves.
- ✓ Thank them for the lessons and memories.
- ✓ Let them go with gratitude – through donation, recycling, or in some cases, respectful disposal like burning in a ritual or burying the items. This act clears space not only in your home, but also in your heart.

Step Two: Clear and Open the Space

Love needs room to breathe. Start in your bedroom – the most intimate space in your home.

- ✓ **Closets & Drawers:** Leave a little empty space. An open shelf or empty drawer sends a signal: *there is space for someone else here.*
- ✓ **Bed Placement:** Position your bed in the command position, where you can see the door but are not directly in line with it. This creates safety and harmony.
- ✓ **Clutter-Free Zone:** Remove stacks of books, exercise equipment, or anything unrelated to rest and romance. Let your bedroom whisper: *love, sanctuary, peace.*

Step Three: Create Pairs and Balance

If everything in your room reflects only you – a single lamp, one pillow, artwork of solitary figures – you may be unconsciously reinforcing aloneness. Shift this by:

- ✓ Placing matching nightstands on either side of the bed.
- ✓ Adding two lamps, two candles, or two chairs.
- ✓ Choosing artwork of pairs – lovers, birds, trees, or any symbol of togetherness.

These visual cues remind both you and the universe: *this is a space for two.*

Step Four: Activate the Partnership Area

Activate the Partnership area on your Magnetic Game Board:

- ✓ Place symbols of love such as pink flowers, rose quartz, or artwork of pairs.
- ✓ Use colors like pink or soft red to invite warmth and affection.
- ✓ Keep this area clear of clutter and avoid storing items that represent loneliness or heaviness.

✓ Place two matching pillows on your bed. Avoid using three of anything.

Step Five: Set the Intention

Every change becomes more powerful when paired with intention. As you arrange your bedroom and activate the Partnership area, declare your desire clearly:

> "I am ready for love. I make space for love.
> Love is welcome in my life now."

Write your intention and tuck it under your pillow, inside a jewelry box, or in the Partnership corner of your home. Let your words ripple through the space.

A Simple Bedroom Ritual for Love

✓ Light two candles in your bedroom – one for yourself and one for your future or current partner.
✓ Place a piece of rose quartz between them.
✓ Speak aloud what you are calling in: love, intimacy, joy, partnership.
✓ Close your eyes and visualize love already present in your life, filling the room with warmth.

> Repeat often. Ritual builds momentum, and
> momentum calls love forward.

Love does not arrive because we chase it. It arrives when we create the space for it to land. By releasing the past, creating balance, and living with intention, you transform your home into a sanctuary where love feels not only possible, it feels like it's inevitable.

A STORY

Opening the Door to Partnership

A few years ago, I worked with a client named Emily. She was ready to call in a committed relationship but felt frustrated because dating seemed to lead nowhere. Her home reflected her inner state: cluttered closets, a nightstand stacked with old journals, and a bedroom that felt more like storage than sanctuary for a couple.

We started with clearing. Emily released gifts, letters, and items tied to past relationships, thanking them for the lessons they brought and making space for what was next. We cleared her bedroom surfaces, rearranged her furniture, and placed her bed in the command position so she could see the door but wasn't directly aligned with it.

Next, we created balance. Matching nightstands, two lamps, and artwork of pairs transformed the energy. We activated her Relationship area with pink flowers, rose quartz, and a framed picture of a couple laughing together – symbols that resonated with the kind of partnership she desired.

Finally, Emily set a clear intention: each morning and evening, she would say, "I am ready for love. I make space for love. Love is welcome in my life now," visualizing herself with her partner, feeling joy and connection.

Within three months, Emily met someone special. She told me later that the first thing she noticed about him was how naturally comfortable he made her feel – almost as if he belonged in her newly harmonized space. They're now building a committed partnership together, and Emily says her home continues to support their love every single day.

Wedding Blessing

The Nine Treasures

This is a beautiful adjustment I have used and love to give clients to call in new love or strengthen their existing relationship with auspicious chi. If you are invited to attend a wedding, gather nine personal items and wrap them in a red cloth. Find a time and respectfully ask the couple to touch each of the nine items. (On their wedding day, the energy of the couple marrying is at an all-time high celebrating their union in the presence of friends and family. In essence they are touching each item imbuing it with the frequency of love and these personal items will hold that energy for you.

How it works:

1. Begin with a square red cloth, nine inches by nine inches. Numbers carry vibration, and nine is the most auspicious of all. It symbolizes completion, wholeness, and eternity. The square represents stability and grounding.

2. On the cloth, place nine personal items – small treasures that you use every day or something in your home that represents partnership. These personal items can be:
    - A watch, jewelry, necklace, anything you wear every day.
    - A coin you keep for prosperity
    - A crystal for clarity and harmony (a pair of crystal dolphins wrapped together in red thread)
    - A small bell or chime for joy
    - A heart-shaped stone for devotion
    - A written prayer for protection
    - A candle for light and guidance
    - A ribbon or thread symbolizing the bond of union

The items don't need to be elaborate; what matters is intention. Each item is something you keep to cultivate this amazing partnership energy into your life.

3. On the wedding day, carry the cloth of nine treasures with you. At an appropriate moment – perhaps after the ceremony or during a quiet blessing circle – invite the bride and groom to touch each item one by one. As their hands connect with the treasures, they imbue your items with partnership energy of love.

4. Take these items home and wear your personal items and place the other items in your home.

The Nine Treasures Blessing is more than a ritual – it is a prayer made tangible, a way to call the highest energies of love, abundance, and joy of the union of these two souls into your life.

Chapter 19

Inviting the Flow of Abundance

Prosperity is more than money. It's about living in the flow of life – where opportunities arrive at the right time, support surrounds you, and there is always more than enough. True prosperity is a dance between gratitude, generosity, and receptivity.

Your home is a mirror of how you allow abundance to flow – or not. Stagnant energy, clutter, or neglect can block the current. Vibrant energy, intentional placement, and symbols of wealth open the river of prosperity wide.

A Quick Conversation About Money

Before we dive into adjusting your home for prosperity, let's have a frank conversation about money. Often, the biggest block to abundance isn't your home – it's you. Your energy around money is only reflected in your space.

When we feel tight on money, 90% of our energy goes to thinking about it. Our thoughts are consumed by scarcity, worry, and what's "enough." But when we feel abundant – confident that we have more than enough to support housing, food, and the things that bring us joy – money only occupies about 10% of our energy.

When you shift from scarcity to abundance that frees up 90% of your energy to use for other things.

Most of us live in a society built on consumerism. Banks know how to keep our finances tight, but manageable. Nine times out of ten, when I work with clients, they express a desire to become debt-free. While this is understandable, repeatedly focusing on the word "debt" with strong emotion actually calls debt to you. The universe responds to the energy we put out.

Now is the time to train your Reticular Activating System (RAS) to focus on savings instead. Begin noticing your savings grow, and make it a game – collecting money, watching it increase, and celebrating the small wins. This creates a cycle of freedom: the more abundant you feel, the more energy you have to do what you love.

Debt is rarely the problem. Think of it as a sign that you are creditworthy. Financial institutions believe in you. In fact, if you had no debt at all, you might not be leveraging the energy of money to create greater prosperity.

Being affluent allows you to energetically be of greater service in the world. You have the means to buy things which creates jobs. You have the capacity to give from an overflowing cup when you see a need. True abundance is about alignment – not scarcity – and your energy, choices, and beliefs create the flow.

The Prosperity Area

On the Magnetic Game Board, the Prosperity area is located in the back left corner of your home when standing at the front door facing inside. This area governs more than financial wealth – it amplifies self-worth, blessings, and your ability to receive.

Ways to activate the Prosperity area:

- ✓ **Healthy Plants:** Lush, vibrant plants symbolize growth and expansion. Avoid dried or struggling plants.
- ✓ **Water Features:** Flowing water represents money and opportunity in motion. A small fountain or an image of water works beautifully.
- ✓ **Symbols of Abundance:** Objects that represent prosperity – coins, crystals, art depicting overflowing bowls, or harvest symbols.
- ✓ **The Color Purple:** Incorporate purple through fabric, art, or decor to invite wealth energy.

Clearing Blockages and Leaks

Before adding anything, clear what blocks abundance. Clutter weighs down opportunity and broken or unused items create financial "leaks." If your bathroom is in the Prosperity area like mine is, use a plant, a bowl of seeds like rice, sesame, mustard seeds or bird seed on the back of the toilet to invite prosperity to come up and nourish the plant or seeds. Use red electrical tape, a red marker, red string or your bottle of Magnetic Red Paint to wrap around on the drainpipe underneath any sinks. You can use red polish or a marker around the drain of the tub and showers.

Ask yourself: Does this area feel like it attracts richness, or does it feel neglected?

Clean, repair, and beautify this space first. A cleared, vibrant Prosperity area sets the foundation for abundance to flow.

Whole-Home Prosperity Adjustments

Prosperity is not limited to one corner. Your entire home contributes to your wealth vibration:

- ✓ **Front Door:** This is where opportunities enter. Keep it clean, inviting, and uncluttered. A strong welcome mat, wreath, or potted plant signals abundance is invited.

✓ **Stove:** The stove represents wealth. Use all burners to activate financial opportunities and keep it clean and in good repair.
✓ **Mirrors:** A mirror reflecting the dining table symbolically doubles your food supply and abundance.

Aligning Inner and Outer Energy

Your home amplifies the energy you hold. If you feel unworthy or fearful around money, the environment reflects that back.

Cultivate a wealth vibration through:

✓ Gratitude for what you already have
✓ Affirmations of worthiness and abundance
✓ Generosity, which opens the flow of giving and receiving

Your home is a tuning fork: when inner belief aligns with your outer environment, prosperity flows naturally.

Prosperity Ritual

Here's a simple ritual to invite abundance:

1. In the Prosperity area, place a small dish with nine coins.
2. Light a candle and speak your intention: "I welcome prosperity, joy, and blessings into my life."
3. Each time you see the dish, touch the coins and affirm abundance.

This ritual activates wealth energy and trains your subconscious to expect prosperity.

A STORY

Prosperity Unlocked

One client, Sarah, came to me frustrated. No matter what she did, her finances felt stuck. Her Prosperity corner had been turned into a storage area – boxes stacked to the ceiling, filled with old tax papers, broken lamps, and unused items. The energy felt heavy, blocked, and forgotten.

Together, we cleared the space, donated what she no longer needed, recycled broken items, and placed a healthy, thriving plant in a purple pot. A small tabletop fountain symbolized money flowing freely.

Within two weeks, Sarah received an unexpected refund check and a surprise job offer with a significant pay increase. More importantly, she said, *"I feel lighter. I feel worthy of money now, like I'm finally open to receive."*

When you align your space with prosperity, you align your life with abundance.

Chapter 20

The Five Elements:

Balancing the Energies of Your Life and Home

At the heart of Chinese philosophy are The Five Elements: Wood, Fire, Earth, Metal, and Water. These elements are not literal in every case – you won't always need a fire burning or a pond indoors – but rather, they are expressions of energy. Each carries its own qualities, shapes, colors, and materials. Together, the Five Elements create balance and harmony in our lives and homes.

The Five Elements aren't only a map for designing harmonious spaces – they are also a philosophy of life itself. In traditional Chinese thought, they describe the way energy flows through our bodies, our emotions, and the world around us. When the elements are in balance, we experience vitality, clarity, and abundance. When one element is out of balance, the flow of Chi becomes blocked, and we may experience illness, struggle, or lack.

The Qualities and Expressions of the Five Elements

- **Wood:** Growth, vitality, vision, expansion
  - *Colors:* Green, teal, blue
  - *Shapes:* Rectangles, tall columns
  - *Representations:* Plants, trees, wooden furniture, bamboo

- **Fire:** Passion, transformation, inspiration, recognition
  - *Colors:* Red, strong pink, purple, orange
  - *Shapes:* Triangles, pointed peaks
  - *Representations:* Candles, lights, fireplaces, art with sun or animals

- **Earth:** Stability, nourishment, grounding, support
  - *Colors:* Yellow, beige, sandy tones, browns
  - *Shapes:* Squares, flat surfaces
  - *Representations:* Bricks, pottery, clay, tiles, natural stone

- **Metal:** Clarity, precision, efficiency, refinement
  - *Colors:* White, gray, metallics (gold, silver, bronze)
  - *Shapes:* Circles, ovals, domes
  - *Representations:* Sculptures, coins, metal frames, bells, chimes

- **Water:** Flow, abundance, wisdom, spirituality
  - *Colors:* Black, deep blue
  - *Shapes:* Curves, wavy lines
  - *Representations:* Fountains, mirrors, glass, art of oceans or rivers.

Cycles of Five Element Energy

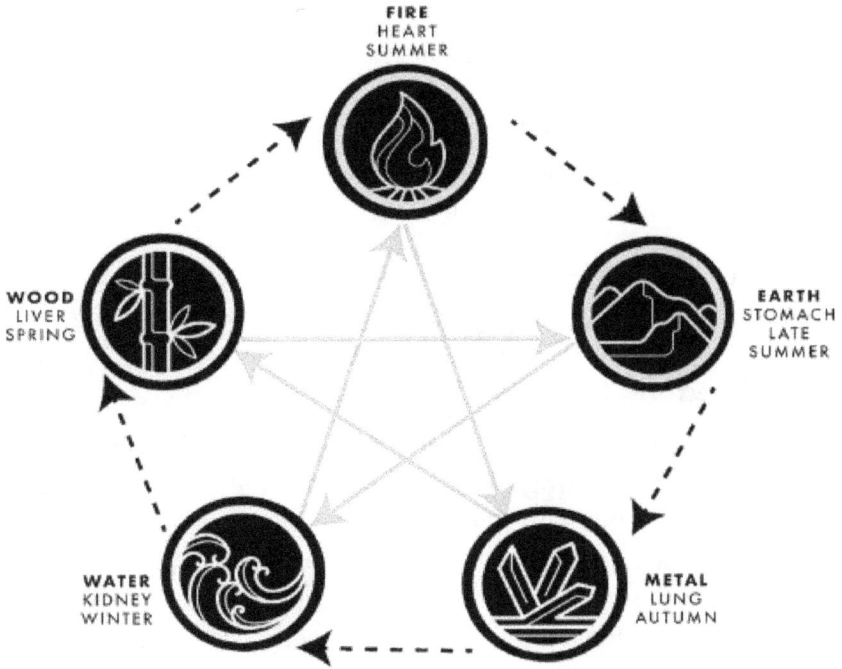

The Five Elements interact in two main ways: the **Constructive Cycle** (which builds and nourishes energy) and the **Destructive Cycle** (which controls and keeps energy in check).

Constructive Cycle

- Wood feeds Fire
- Fire creates Earth (ash)
- Earth produces Metal (minerals)
- Metal carries Water (condensation)
- Water nourishes Wood

This cycle creates flow, growth, and harmony when all elements are represented and balanced.

Destructive Cycle

- Wood breaks through Earth (roots disrupting soil)
- Earth dams Water
- Water extinguishes Fire
- Fire melts Metal
- Metal cuts Wood

This cycle is not "bad." It brings necessary control and checks to keep energy from becoming overwhelming.

Creating Harmony in Home and Life

A home with too much of one element without balance can be overwhelming. Imagine a cabin filled with wood paneling, wood beams, and wooden rustic furniture – it may feel heavy and stagnant. Because there is so much of the Wood element, adding some Fire elements such as fireplaces, red, or triangle shapes helps deplete the Wood energy. Metal elements such as the color white and oval shapes help to cut the swampy, stagnant feel. You definitely would not want to add Water elements because Water feeds Wood and it would only magnify the intensity of the Wood energy.

Or picture a home with endless glass, chrome, and white surfaces. It would most likely feel very sterile unless it is warmed with Earth elements such as brick or pottery and earth tones. Or it could be enlivened with Wood, the color green, plants and wooden objects.

Shapes of homes themselves reflect this philosophy. A tall, narrow building emphasizes Wood energy. A wide, flat ranch-style home carries Earth energy. A home with sharp peaks in its roofline holds Fire energy. Each shape influences how people feel and thrive inside. When building a new home, it's also important to consider the land and what element energy is there: wood, water, mountains.

When your home holds all five in harmony, you feel supported in health, relationships, and abundance. And when one is out of balance, both your environment and your body often reflect it – whether through stress, lack of vitality, or financial struggle.

Balancing a Home Through the Elements

When you enter a space, you may notice that one element is overpowering. For example:

- ✓ A home filled with tall plants, rectangular shapes, and green tones may feel like "too much wood." This can create restless or overwhelming growth energy. Adding Fire (candles, lights) can transform the excess Wood into dynamic movement, or introducing Metal can help cut through and refine it.
- ✓ A room painted entirely red with many triangular patterns may feel overstimulating due to excess Fire. Water elements – like a mirror, glass, or deep blues – can help cool and balance it.
- ✓ A heavy Earth environment – lots of beige, square shapes, and stone – can feel stagnant or stuck. Adding Wood energy (plants, vertical lines, greens) can lift and enliven the space.

The Shape of Homes and Environments

Even the architecture of your home or the landscape around it is influenced by the Five Elements:

- ✓ A **tall, narrow house** reflects strong Wood energy.
- ✓ A home with sharp angles or triangular rooflines carries Fire energy.
- ✓ A **low, square building** radiates Earth energy.
- ✓ A round or dome-shaped house emphasizes Metal.
- ✓ A home near a river, lake, or with curved architecture carries Water energy.

When a home is dominated by one shape or material, the other elements can be brought in intentionally through color, furniture, art, and décor to restore balance.

The wisdom of the Five Elements is that no element stands alone. Just like in nature, they are always interacting, building, and tempering one another. By consciously weaving them into your home, you create harmony not only in your environment, but also in your inner world – because your space is a mirror of your soul's vibration.

The Five Elements in Health and Abundance

The Five Elements aren't only a map for designing harmonious spaces – they are also a philosophy of life itself. In traditional Chinese thought, they describe the way energy flows through our bodies, our emotions, and the world around us. When the elements are in balance, we experience vitality, clarity, and abundance. When one element is out of balance, the flow of Chi becomes blocked, and we may experience illness, struggle, or lack.

The Elements and the Body

- Wood – Connected to the liver and gallbladder.
    - Emotions: Anger, frustration, drive, vision
    - Balanced Wood energy helps us make decisions, plan for the future, and grow. When blocked, it shows up as irritability, impatience, or feeling "stuck."
- Fire – Connected to the heart and small intestine.
    - Emotions: Joy, passion, anxiety
    - Balanced Fire energy brings warmth, enthusiasm, and inspiration. Too much Fire may cause restlessness, burnout, or anxiety.
- Earth – Connected to the stomach and spleen.
    - Emotions: Worry, sympathy, groundedness
    - Balanced Earth provides nourishment, stability, and security. When out of balance, it may

manifest as overthinking, worry, or digestive issues.
- Metal – Connected to the lungs and large intestine.
  - Emotions: Grief, clarity, discipline
  - Balanced Metal gives us focus, discernment, and the ability to let go. Blocked Metal can show up as rigidity, sadness, or holding on to the past.
- Water – Connected to the kidneys and bladder.
  - Emotions: Fear, wisdom, calm
  - Balanced Water gives us courage, intuition, and a sense of flow. Too much fear or exhaustion often indicates weak Water energy.

When your home supports all Five Elements, it also supports these systems within your body – nourishing your health on a physical and emotional level.

The Five Elements and Abundance

Abundance is not just about money – it is about energy flowing into your life with ease. The Five Elements act as a map for how that energy circulates:

- **Wood** energy represents **growth and vision** – it's the seed of new ideas and opportunities. Without Wood, there is no beginning.
- **Fire** energy represents **visibility and recognition** – it's when your work or presence shines so that abundance can find you.
- **Earth** energy represents **stability and trust** – the ground that supports prosperity. Without Earth, abundance can't take root.
- **Metal** energy represents **clarity and value** – the ability to define your worth and attract resources.
- **Water** energy represents **flow and wisdom** – the circulation of wealth, opportunities, and support in your life.

When one of these is missing, prosperity feels blocked. For example:

- ✓ You may have brilliant ideas (Wood) but if Fire is missing, no one sees them.
- ✓ You may be visible and recognized (Fire) but without Earth, the success feels shaky and doesn't last.
- ✓ You may have stability (Earth) but without Water, money and opportunities don't circulate.

The key is not to have equal amounts of each, but to have **flow between them** – so that your health, home, and prosperity move in harmony.

And one of my favorites if you are really wanting to put some high energy into your work or abundance, Fire + Water = Steam. Sometimes, I intentionally wear red and black together for this reason.

Chapter 21

Manifesting at Hyper Speed

Being an avid student and teacher of manifesting and feng shui for over 25 years, I have come across countless ways to call in what you truly desire. While there are many approaches, the simplest and most powerful method for me always comes back to three key steps:

1. Get Clear on What You Want
2. Ask for It (out loud or in writing)
3. Go into the Quantum Field

Most of us are not clear on what we want. The Universe is always listening and responding to your energy; if you are like most people, it's receiving a static signal. Whether you realize it or not, your message is likely jumbled – unclear or changing moment to moment.

When you take the time to get clear on what you want and clearly state your desire consistently, you come across loud and clear setting the energetic wheels in motion. This concept is echoed even in sacred texts like the Bible: when you ask, it is given. That defines free will.

The third step is where the magic truly begins: entering the Quantum Field, the unseen energetic space of infinite potential.

This is the sparkly, vibrant force of nature – the energy that flows through all things. When you engage with this field consciously, you can see, feel, and sense opportunities aligning with your intention. It's not about forcing outcomes; that just leaves you tired or at a cost of energy. It's about creating energetic space so that inspiration and action flow naturally. This is how I've manifested the life I live today.

The Four Domains of Manifesting

In my studies and hands-on practice, I have consistently observed the Four Domains of Manifesting™ at play. Manifestation is not a single action or one-time ritual – it is a synergy of these four guiding principles that work together to bring your desires into reality. Understanding and applying these domains ensures that your energy, intention, and actions are fully aligned with your highest path.

These Four Domains are an incredible manifesting blueprint I want to leave you with, the framework that allows you to harness the Universe's energy with clarity, purpose, and joy. Master these principles, and you'll see how effortless, yet profound, the process of manifesting can truly be.

DOMAIN #1

The Law of Vibration

The very foundation of manifesting is vibration. Long before we see results in the outer world, energy begins shifting in the unseen. The Law of Vibration teaches us that everything – our thoughts, emotions, bodies, homes, and even the food we eat – holds a frequency. That frequency either draws in more of what we desire or pushes it away.

Most people have heard of the Law of Attraction, but few understand that it rests on the Law of Vibration. You don't attract what you want – you attract what you are in vibrational harmony with. If your energy is heavy with doubt, fear, or worry, you will call in more of the same. If your energy is uplifted, inspired, and tuned to joy, opportunities and synchronicities flow with ease.

Keeping your energy up is not about pretending everything is perfect. It's about cultivating practices that raise your frequency, steady your emotional state, and return you to alignment quickly when life gets messy.

Rather than dwelling in self-doubt and worry, it's about developing the tools and the "muscle" to take your focus off your current difficulties and bring your focus into the alignment of what it is that you want to create next. Worry is such a low-level emotion. The only things you can manifest from here are more things to worry about. Authenticity, joy, gratitude, having fun, doing what you love are the vibrational states that make you ultra-magnetic.

The Emotional Guidance Scale

One of the simplest ways to measure vibration is through emotion. Emotions are guidance, they tell you instantly where your frequency is. Joy, gratitude, and love vibrate at the highest frequency. Anger, fear, and despair vibrate much lower.

When you know where you are on the Emotional Guidance Scale, you gain the power to shift. The goal is not to leap from despair to bliss in a single moment. It's to advance one or two steps at a time and maintain that frequency. If you are constantly switching from grief and despair to joy and back to depression, that is manic. It's a kind of rollercoaster you don't want to be on. Instead, if you are in an emotional state of worry, moving to frustration is an improvement. Frustration is a positive vibration. From there, you can move to hope, then optimism, then joy. Slow and steady.

When you feel better, your vibration rises. And when your vibration rises, life responds in kind.

The Emotional Guidance Scale is a tool developed by Abraham-Hicks to help you understand and navigate your

177

emotions as a form of energetic feedback. Your emotions are not just feelings – they are signals from your inner being about how aligned you are with your desires and your true self. I like to think of emotion as energy in motion.

By learning to read these signals and move intentionally up the scale, you can shift your vibration, raise your energy, and manifest what you truly want with more ease and flow.

Emotion	Level	
Joy/Love/Empowerment/Authenticity/Gratitude	1	
Passion	2	
Enthusiasm/Eagerness/Happiness	3	
Positive Expectation/Belief	4	
Optimism	5	
Hopefulness	6	
Contentment	7	🙂
Boredom	8	
Pessimism	9	
Frustration/Irritation/Impatience	10	
Overwhelment	11	
Disappointment	12	
Doubt	13	
Worry	14	
Blame	15	🙁
Discouragement	16	
Anger	17	
Revenge	18	
Hatred/Rage	19	
Jealousy	20	
Insecurity/Guilt/Unworthiness	21	
Fear/Grief/Depression/Despair/Powerlessness	22	

Abraham Hicks organizes emotions from lowest to highest vibration, showing a clear path from feeling "bad" to feeling "good":

Fear / Grief / Depression / Despair / Powerlessness

- The lowest end of the scale.
- Indicates complete misalignment with your inner being.
- Energy is heavy, stagnant, and resistant.

Insecurity / Guilt / Unworthiness /Jealousy / Hatred/ Rage / Revenge

- Still heavy, but you are starting to notice your resistance.
- You see others who have what you want.
- It can spark moments of clarity.

Anger / Discouragement / Blame /Worry

- Common, everyday resistance points.
- These feelings signal that you are aware of what you want but not yet fully aligned.
- You think there is something outside of yourself you need that you don't have.

Doubt / Disappointment /Overwhelment / Frustration / Irritation / Impatience / Pessimism

- Middle of the scale
- You are working hard to get what you want.
- It's not happening fast enough or more is happening and you need to regulate the flow.
- These emotions indicate an opportunity to pivot perspective.

Boredom / Contentment / Hopefulness / Optimism / Positive Expectation / Belief

- You have reached a positive vibration.
- Energy is flowing; manifestation is closer.
- You are working hard to get what you want and it's not happening fast enough or more is happening and you need to regulate to the flow.

Enthusiasm / Eagerness / Happiness / Passion / Freedom

- High vibration.
- You are intentionally guiding your energy toward what you want.
- The universe is responding in alignment.

Joy / Love / Empowerment / Authenticity / Gratitude

- The highest end of the scale.
- Emotions here indicate complete alignment with your inner being.
- Manifestation flows effortlessly.

How to Use the Emotional Guidance Scale

1. **Identify Where You Are:**
   - Check in with your emotions. Which word or feeling best represents your current state?

2. **Allow Movement:**
   - Don't try to jump from fear to joy immediately – that creates resistance and manic emotions.
   - Move slowly step by step, choosing slightly better-feeling thoughts each time.
   - As an example, if you are depressed, see if you can move to jealousy. If you are jealous, move to anger. Get angry! Say all the bad words. It's a higher vibrational state than depression, guilt or jealousy.

3. **Shift Your Focus:**
   - Use affirmations, gratitude, or visualization to move up the scale.

4. **Even a small lift in emotion signals alignment. Notice Your Progress:**
   - Every time you feel a better-feeling thought, recognize it.
   - Hold that vibration steady, until you are ready to move to the next vibrational level.
   - Momentum builds as your vibration rises.

Tips for Daily Practice

- ✓ **Morning Check-In:** Start your day by noticing how you feel and setting the intention to move upward on the scale.
- ✓ **Journaling:** Write down your current emotion and one thought that feels slightly better. Track your progress.
- ✓ **Home Energy Alignment:** Use your space to support movement up the scale – declutter, bring in colors, objects, or Solfeggio frequencies that lift your vibration.
- ✓ **Micro-Shifts:** Even tiny improvements in emotion matter. A small spark of hope or curiosity can begin a powerful upward flow.

Your emotions are your *compass* – not your enemy. Low-vibration feelings aren't "bad"; they are clues, showing you what you want to release and what to move toward. The goal isn't perfection – it's momentum, alignment, and joy.

Notice that guilt is an incredibly low vibration. If you find yourself feeling guilty often, then really look into that and why you have been holding on to that. Let it go. And jealousy. If you are jealous of someone, get curious. Jealousy is an indication that they have something you want. Maybe it's a relationship, or their flawless skin, or their ability to travel. Shift to excitement. Because if they can have it, you can have it, too. I make a habit of being really happy for people to get what they want. I celebrate their success with them. I'm truly happy for everyone who has good things happening for them, especially if my life might be temporarily off. I see their good fortune as my good fortune.

By practicing awareness and conscious movement up the scale, you can have so much more peace, love and joy in your own life. And practice being true to yourself. Authenticity is a high vibration, and it is the magic sauce to manifesting what you want with greater speed and accuracy.

The Mirror Exercise

If you suffer from any of the lower vibrations like insecurity, guilt, depression or powerlessness, I highly, highly recommend The Mirror Exercise.

Take five minutes a day for 30 days (mark it on your calendar) and simply look at yourself in the mirror. Connect to yourself through your eyes. You may find it difficult at first but stick with it. Allow any emotions to come up. If there are tears, let them flow. If there is anger, be angry. Most people don't prioritize this because they don't think it is working. Oh, it is working alright. This is not silliness; this is life changing.

I don't know how it works, but at the end of the month, if you've done this consistently, you will love and appreciate yourself more. And your self-worth will have increased.

Everyday Things You Can Do to Raise Your Vibration

Here are a few practices I love – and that I've taught to hundreds of clients – to keep the energy high and aligned with what you want to manifest.

Smile Big

It sounds almost silly, but your physiology impacts your vibration. Smiling – even when you don't feel like it – sends signals to your brain that life is safe, good, and worth enjoying. A big smile instantly lifts your energy. Try it right now and notice the shift. The nice thing is that smiling is contagious. You can't smile at someone and not have them smile back. This shifts their frequency, too.

Take Your Shoes Off and Stand on the Earth.

When energy feels chaotic, grounding restores balance. Go outside, stand barefoot on the earth, and let your energy roots sink deep. This practice calms your nervous system and steadies your frequency by releasing energy into the earth. We have an energetic connection to the earth and now that most of us are wearing rubber-soled shoes, that connection is lost.

Play Solfeggio Frequencies

Certain sounds carry specific vibrations that harmonize your energy. Solfeggio tones – ancient frequencies once used in sacred music – can clear blocks, open intuition, and raise your vibration. Play them in the background as you work, meditate, or sleep. Your home will love it, too! I've included a whole section on this at the end of the chapter.

Cook with Intention.

Food carries energy, and so does the cook. When you prepare meals with love, gratitude, and joy, that frequency infuses the food and nourishes more than just the body, it uplifts the spirit. Stirring your soup while silently affirming, *"May this meal bring energy, health, and happiness to all who eat it,"* transforms cooking into a manifesting practice.

When you integrate these practices – emotional awareness, grounding, smiling, sound frequencies, cooking with intention, affirmations, and vision walls – you begin to live at a higher frequency. This doesn't mean life becomes perfect, but it does become magnetic.

The Universe responds to vibration with precision. As you keep your energy up, aligned, and intentional, you discover that manifesting isn't about forcing or chasing. It's about becoming a vibrational match to what you desire.

Your joy, your peace, your clarity – they are not luxuries. They are the very frequency of creation.

More Energy-Shifting Actions

- ✓ **Create Vision Points.** Display symbols of love, abundance, health, and joy in key places around your home. These focal points act like mini vision boards. For example, when I wanted my children to have a close bond, I framed photos of them together in frames that said "friends."
- ✓ **Release the Shoulds.** Remove items that carry negative memories – even if they come from someone

you love. Keeping things out of guilt or obligation only ties you to old energy. Give them to someone who will appreciate them or donate.

✓ **Make Your Bedroom Sacred.** Your bedroom should feel like a sanctuary, not a storage unit. Remove exercise equipment, work papers, clutter under the bed, TVs, and mirrors. Close bathroom doors at night. Position your bed so it feels supportive and calming.

✓ **Carve Out Sacred Space.** Even if it's a small corner with a chair, candle, and cushion, create a space where you can meditate, reflect, or simply *be*.

✓ **Do More of What You Love.** Dance in your living room, meditate, play in the garden, or do something wildly creative. Joyful energy always amplifies your personal vibration.

DOMAIN #2

Reticular Cells

There's a tiny part of your brain that acts like a filter for reality. It's called the Reticular Activating System (RAS). Think of it as your brain's search engine. Whatever you give attention to, your RAS starts scanning the world for evidence of it.

Have you ever thought about buying a certain car – and suddenly, you see it everywhere? That's your RAS in action. The cars were always there, but your awareness wasn't tuned to notice them until your focus shifted.

When you understand how to work with your RAS, you unlock one of the most powerful tools in manifesting. You train your brain to look for what you want, rather than what you fear.

Your RAS is like a bridge between the conscious and subconscious mind. The subconscious mind holds patterns, beliefs, and memories that drive much of your behavior. The conscious mind sets goals, desires, and intentions. The RAS links them by bringing opportunities into awareness that align with your focus.

If you focus on problems, your RAS will highlight more problems. If you focus on solutions, abundance, and alignment, your RAS will deliver evidence of them in your daily life.

This is why I say: your focus is your frequency.

Journaling: Training the RAS

One of the most effective ways to direct your RAS is through journaling. When you write down what you want – clearly, consistently, and with feeling – you program your mind to search for it.

Try this: each morning, write 3–5 statements beginning with *"I am..."* or *"I have..."* For example:

- I am living in a beautiful home that nourishes me.
- I have aligned clients who value my work.

- I am open to unexpected opportunities for joy and prosperity.

The act of writing signals to your RAS: *this is important, find it.*

Future Visioning

When I am unclear of the direction, I am going next, I start writing about my future consistently. I will write stories about how I want my life to look 18 months from today. I will take 10 to 15 minutes to write quickly without editing myself. I keep a notebook specifically for this. In another section, I write my three to seven intentions daily for what I want to manifest and by when.

I love listening to Joe Dispenza meditations on YouTube when I first wake up (when my energy is most connected to the Quantum Field) and visualize what I want to have happen.

Journaling is the most powerful way I know to get clear on what I want. Sometimes, I write things I have never even considered. It's interesting to go back and review what I have written in previous years. My message has always been consistent, teach Manifesting Feng Shui and design incredible spaces. However, all too often, I have gotten distracted and veered off my path.

The Universe always has a way of bringing me back to what I truly love and feel authentically designed to do, have and be.

Vision Boards, Vision Walls, and Mirrors

Your RAS responds to images as much as words. This is why vision boards are so popular – they give your subconscious a visual cue. But I love to take it further:

- **Vision Board**: A personal collage of images and words that represent your desires. Keep it in a place where you'll see it often.
- **Vision Wall**: A vision wall is a place that you see frequently. It can be at the foot of your bed where you see at night before you go to sleep or first thing when you

wake up in the morning. It can also be the wall that you look at while you are sitting at your desk. It's an ideal place to hang your vision board and other reminders about what you want to manifest.

- **Mirror Affirmations**: By writing affirmations directly on your bathroom mirror or in your shower with a dry erase marker (just make sure your shower tile isn't porous), you integrate vision into your daily routine. Your reflection becomes paired with your future self. The shower is another great place to visualize what it is that you want to manifest.

Each of these practices trains your RAS by flooding it with visual and verbal evidence of what you're creating.

Affirmations on Steroids

More than affirmations, these statements really trick your mind into calling in what you desire.

What would I do if I had everything I ever wanted?

Placing this statement in key places like your car, on your nightstand, next to your bathroom mirror, on the cover of your notebook, actually trick the mind. While you are asking what you would do, you are also automatically assuming you have everything you ever wanted and so things start naturally shifting and soon enough you are doing so much more of what you want to be doing.

Getting Rid of Your Big But

So much of the time while we are affirming what we want to have our mind is secretly sabotaging us with, "Yeah, but…" That "but" actually tunes out your RAS. Using "but" between two thoughts negates the first part of the sentence. Your RAS believes that you can't have it so no worries in showing you the opportunity. Turn your "but" into "and" and watch your life shift in the most magical ways. Try it out and see if you can *feel* the difference.

"I want to receive $100,000 or more a year doing what I love, but I have three kids to take care of."

Or "I want to receive $100,000 or more a year AND I have three kids to take care of."

Can you feel the difference? The first one is telling yourself you can't do it because you have kids, and the 2nd one says, "Hmmm, I can receive $100,000 with kids. It might be more challenging, but it's totally doable. Let's get to work on this."

Here's another example.

"I love you, but it drives me crazy when you leave dirty dishes in the sink."

Or "I love you and it drives me crazy when you leave dirty dishes in the sink."

A STORY

Focus on What You Want

One of my clients, Sarah, was stuck in a cycle of lack. She journaled about bills, repeated affirmations about debt, and constantly scanned for what was missing. Not surprisingly, her RAS kept showing her proof of scarcity.

When she shifted to journaling her desires, creating a vision wall in her bedroom, and reframing her language from "but" to "and," everything changed. Within months, she noticed new opportunities, unexpected income, and supportive relationships flowing in. Her external world shifted the moment her internal focus shifted.

The RAS and Higher Consciousness

When combined with practices like meditation, visioning, and intention-setting, the RAS becomes more than a neurological filter – it becomes a spiritual ally. By attuning your brain to notice synchronicities, divine nudges, and subtle alignments, you create a bridge between human consciousness and higher consciousness.

This is why vision walls and affirmations are so powerful. They don't just program the brain; they open portals of awareness to possibilities that already exist in the quantum field. You just have to allow yourself to tap in.

Your RAS doesn't just find what you focus on – it expands your vision so you can see what was hidden in plain sight.

DOMAIN #3

Divine Guidance

Regardless of your religious beliefs, at some point on the manifesting journey, you realize you're not doing this alone. There is a higher wisdom that whispers, nudges, and sometimes shouts to get your attention. I call this Divine Guidance.

Divine Guidance can show up in many forms – a sudden knowing, a feeling in your gut, an inner voice, or an external synchronicity that feels too perfect to ignore. The key is learning to recognize it and trust it.

Divine Guidance is available to all of us. The problem is that we just don't ask for what we want. We just put our heads down and work harder, lowering our vibration, and making it even more difficult to hear those nudges.

Imagine that you have an entire team on the other side of the veil anxiously waiting for you to ask. But you don't. So, they are bored over there. And, like a kid bored in school, they sometimes miss the cue when the teacher is talking to them.

Well, that's you and your Divine Guidance team. The trick is to keep them engaged. Ask them to do things for you, often. When they realize that you are going to be continually asking for things (they love to help!) you've got their full attention.

The more and more you ask, the better you are at hearing the signs and the more manifesting power you have at your disposal.

Ask and It is Given

Like many entrepreneurs, I've known both the sweetness of success and the sting of failure. In 2008, my world came crashing down – my real estate business crashed, I faced bankruptcy, foreclosure, and a painful divorce. I was unemployed, sending out over 200 résumés with no response, and even relying on food shelves to get by.

Then one night after putting my three kids to bed, everything changed. Sitting on the couch looking through the classifieds, frustrated by jobs I didn't want, I had a moment of clarity: *I wanted something I could sell that I believed in 100%.* I stood up and said out loud, "God, bring me something worthy of who I am. I want something I believe in 100% that I can sell."

A week later, the phone rang. A friend offered me an opportunity. At first, it didn't look right – too little money, too much time away from my kids. But a voice inside kept saying, *"This is what you asked for."* So, I trusted, and I jumped all in.

That leap changed everything. In just three years, I helped grow that company from $500,000 to $50 million. I wrote a tagline that repositioned the brand, redesigned the website that boosted sales by 41%, and created a newspaper ad that brought in $60,000 a day – featured in the *New York Times, Wall Street Journal,* and *USA Today.*

That momentum financed a national infomercial, and to my surprise, I was chosen to host it. Soon after, I was one of the top three infomercial hosts in the country.

The best part was that it was something I believed in 100%. I had been in two car accidents by the time I was 25. For years I suffered from terrible neck pain and a lack of mobility in turning my neck. I had even invested in an $11,000 medical device for relief. And nothing I had ever tried worked as well as this $50 pillow. It had a 10-year warranty and a 60-Day money back guarantee. It was an easy sell for me, and I was changing lives by the thousands.

The best part was, I was finally getting good sleep. That changed everything.

From rock bottom to national recognition in just a few years – I proved to myself what's possible when clarity, vision, and asking God align. The truth is, we can manifest extraordinary results when we commit fully to follow the lead of inspiration.

Angel Pages

One of my favorite practices for connecting with Divine Guidance is something I call *Angel Pages*. This is a simple but profound journaling technique. Each morning, before your day fills with noise, sit down with a notebook.

This one may or may not take a bit of practice. I've been doing it for years, so I don't know how long it took to really get in this flow and knowing distinctly which voice is yours and which is the one of Divine Guidance. I can tell you this, they talk very sweetly to me. They are very encouraging and insightful.

I start by writing." Dear Angels, thank you for..."

Then let your pen move. Don't overthink. Don't censor. Just write. (I rarely get more than two sentences written and a flood of thoughts and ideas come to me.)

Sometimes you'll get a page of encouragement. Sometimes you'll get clarity on a decision. And sometimes, you'll receive messages that feel like they didn't come from you at all. That's the beauty of it – you're giving Spirit a channel to speak through.

Increasing Your Intuition

We all have intuition, but like a muscle, it strengthens with use. The more you practice listening, the clearer it becomes. Intuition often shows up as a quiet voice beneath the noise of the Monkey Mind. It feels calm, steady, and true.

Here are some ways to build your intuitive connection:

- **Ask simple questions** throughout the day: "Should I turn left, or right?" "Does this feel expansive or constricting?"
- **Pay attention to your body.** Your body is a tuning fork. A yes will feel light and open; a no will feel heavy or contracted. We often hold the answers in our shoulders, our gut, or if you are like me, you get full-on goosebumps which always means a clear *YES, you are on the right track.*
- **Meditate regularly.** Silence makes it easier to distinguish intuition from random thought. Over time your higher self-voice will completely drown out your small self-talk.

The more you honor your intuition, the louder it speaks.

Oracle Cards

Oracle cards are another doorway into Divine Guidance. They work because they bypass the logical mind. When you shuffle and pull a card, the message that comes forward often mirrors exactly what you need to hear.

It's not the card itself that holds power, it's the alignment between your energy, the question in your heart, and the archetype or symbol on the card.

For example, while writing this very book, I pulled cards that spoke directly to the process: *Solitude, Fulfillment of Wishes, Material & Spiritual Destiny, and Crown Chakra.* Each was a reminder that writing is not just an act of discipline, it's a soul journey guided by Spirit.

Pendulum

A pendulum is a simple tool, but incredibly effective. It's often just a chain with a crystal or weight at the end. You hold it steady and ask a yes-or-no question. The pendulum moves in response to subtle shifts in your own energy field – an extension of your subconscious and your guides.

The pendulum isn't about predicting the future; it's about confirming what you already sense. It's a tangible way to see your intuition in action.

Your Divine Guidance Team is very playful. So, make sure you are having fun connecting with them. Call on them often and you will see the influence they can have at bringing wonderful opportunities you way.

Free Will and Divine Timing

Here's something important: Divine Guidance doesn't override your free will. You are always the creator of your life. Guidance can point you toward opportunities, but you must choose to act.

And sometimes, what you ask for doesn't arrive in your timing. That doesn't mean Spirit isn't listening. It may mean the timing isn't aligned yet, or that something even better is coming. Trust that Divine Timing is part of the process. That brings me to one of my favorite reminders:

God is always working in my favor.

Manifesting requires detachment from the outcome. Yes, you believe and play big like setting big goals, but don't get attached to how it turns out.

A STORY

Angel Pages

One of my clients, Marissa, was torn between two career paths. She journaled, meditated, and still felt unclear. We introduced Angel Pages into her daily practice. Within a week, she began receiving clear guidance – phrases like, *"Follow the path that lights your heart, not the one that pleases others."*

She also began using a pendulum to confirm her intuitive hits. As she leaned into trust, synchronicities began lining up: a conversation with a stranger, an unexpected email, an invitation that aligned perfectly with her heart's desire.

She realized she was never alone. Guidance had always been there, waiting for her to listen.

Living With Divine Guidance

When you cultivate Divine Guidance, your life shifts from effort to flow. You begin to see signs, synchronicities, and nudges as natural parts of your day. Decisions become easier because you feel supported. Manifestations happen faster because you're moving in alignment, not against the current.

The truth is, Divine Guidance isn't reserved for the "gifted." It's available to all of us. The more you invite it, the more it shows up. Inspired means *In Spirit*. I lead an inspired life. I'm not religious, but I am faithful. I keep the connection, and inspiration is a common occurrence in my life. It can be in yours, too.

Domain #4

Free Will

One of the greatest gifts we are given in this lifetime is free will – the ability to choose how we direct our energy, our attention, and our actions. The Universe is constantly flowing with energy, offering us opportunities, synchronicities, and nudges of guidance. But how we respond, how we align, and which path we choose is entirely up to us.

The Law of Vibration teaches us that energy is always moving. Free will is our steering wheel – we get to choose where that energy flows. Every thought, every word, every action is a choice point. When we choose with clarity and authenticity, the Universe responds by amplifying that vibration.

Authenticity as the Compass

Free will does not mean doing whatever we think others expect from us. It is about aligning with our authentic self – the part of us that knows what lights us up, what feels expansive, and what pulls us closer to our burning desires.

Your burning desire is not random. It is the roadmap to your soul purpose. When you follow what you truly long for – not what society tells you to want, not what family expects, but what makes your heart beat faster, you are using your free will to align with your soul's highest path.

Choosing Your Energy

At every moment, you have a choice:

- Do I focus on fear or possibility?
- Do I react out of habit, or respond with intention?
- Do I dim my light to fit in, or shine brightly in truth?

These choices are small in the moment but monumental in impact. Free will gives us the power to shift our vibration instantly. A smile, a word of gratitude, a single act of courage – these are all conscious choices that direct Universal energy in our favor.

Partnership with the Universe

Think of the Universe as a river of flowing energy. You cannot stop the current, but with free will, you can choose your vessel, your direction, and how you ride the waves. When you resist, you create struggle. When you flow with authenticity and desire, the river carries you exactly where you need to go.

"Everything you want is downstream."

~Abraham Hicks

Free will is not about control – it's about alignment. You choose the vibration, and the Universe amplifies it.

Your soul purpose is already written in the energy of your being. Free will is the key that unlocks it. By choosing authenticity, you align with your burning desire, and by aligning with your desire, you step fully into the destiny your soul came here to live.

Chapter 22

Solfeggio Frequencies

Our homes are more than walls and furniture – they are energetic fields that mirror our thoughts, emotions, and intentions. One of the most profound ways to enhance the energy of your space is through sound and vibration, particularly the ancient Solfeggio frequencies.

The History of Solfeggio Frequencies

Solfeggio frequencies are a set of musical tones used for thousands of years in sacred chants and meditation practices, most famously in Gregorian chants of the Middle Ages. These tones were believed to create spiritual, mental, and physical harmony.

432 Hz – The Natural Tuning Frequency

As modern music evolved, the tuning standard shifted from 432 Hz to 440 Hz, slightly altering natural resonance. 440 Hz does feel a little "sharper," more tense in the body. Some sound healers and researchers suggest it subtly disrupts harmony, pulling us away from our natural state.

Many sound healers recommend returning to 432 Hz or Solfeggio-based frequencies to align more fully with the body's natural vibration and promote healing. While modern music is tuned to 440 Hz, many healers and researchers advocate 432 Hz for its alignment with natural resonance.

Why 432 Hz Matters:
- Resonates naturally with the human body and universe
- Promotes cellular harmony and relaxation
- Reduces stress and supports coherent brainwave patterns
- Enhances intuition, creativity, and energetic alignment
- Creates subtle yet powerful shifts in the home's vibration

Think of it as tuning an instrument – if one string is slightly off, the whole sound feels off, even if you don't notice. Homes and bodies are similar: when vibration aligns, energy flows effortlessly.

Frequencies, Resonance, and Health

Everything in the universe vibrates – from our cells to our homes. Exposure to harmonious frequencies can:

- Calm the nervous system, reducing stress and anxiety
- Support emotional balance and mental clarity
- Stimulate the body's natural healing mechanisms
- Make spaces feel lighter, more expansive, and inviting

The core Solfeggio frequencies include:

- **396 Hz** – Liberates guilt and fear
- **417 Hz** – Facilitates change and clears obstacles
- **528 Hz** – Transformation and miracles, including DNA repair
- **639 Hz** – Enhances relationships and connection
- **741 Hz** – Awakens intuition
- **852 Hz** – Returns balance and spiritual order

Conversely, dissonant or chaotic frequencies can create tension, fatigue, and stagnant energy both in the body and in the home.

Using Sound to Create a Magnetic Home

You can transform your home into a magnetic, harmonious environment by using sound intentionally:

- ✓ **Background Music:** Play tones or ambient music tuned to 432 Hz or Solfeggio frequencies to subtly align energy throughout your space.
- ✓ **Meditation & Chanting:** Use Solfeggio tones during meditation to activate Prosperity, Love, or Career energy in corresponding Life Areas
- ✓ **Objects that Resonate:** Singing bowls, tuning forks, chimes, or bells physically move stagnant energy and raise the frequency of a space.

Room-Specific Frequencies:

- **Bedroom:** 528 Hz – healing, rejuvenation, emotional restoration
- **Living Area:** 639 Hz – connection, positive relationships
- **Office:** 417 Hz – clarity, productive energy, change
- **Prosperity Area:** 396 Hz – release financial blocks and invite abundance

Even small, consistent exposure can subtly raise the vibration of your entire home, making it a magnetic sanctuary of health, joy, and abundance.

Chapter 23

Homes Styled by Inspiration

Every home has a personality, just like the people who live in it. Now that you've discovered what you love – your treasures, your favorite colors, the items that spark joy – it's time to let your home reflect your unique energy. Styling isn't just about aesthetics; it's about creating a space that feels alive, harmonious, and aligned with your soul.

Some homes are full of life and energy, like Georgia's, bustling with color, vibrant textures, and conversation-starting pieces. Others are quiet sanctuaries, calm and meditative, offering rest and grounding after a long day. No matter what your style, your home can become a magnetic reflection of you.

Styling for Vibrancy and Energy

If your home personality leans toward bold, expressive, and full of life:

- **Colors & Artwork:** Use bright, popping colors and artwork that excites your senses. Think vibrant throw pillows, statement wall art, or a colorful rug.
- **Statement Pieces:** Place one eye-catching piece in each room – a sculpture, lamp, or unique piece of furniture. Even a corner can become a focal point that makes the room feel larger and more dynamic.

- **Plants & Life:** Mix plant varieties with different heights, textures, and colorful pots to amplify energy. Flowers or plants in bright ceramic pots can energize your living areas.
- **Flow & Cohesion:** Keep energy flowing from room to room by repeating colors, patterns, or materials in different spaces. This creates visual harmony without dulling your energy.

Styling for Calm and Sanctuary

If your home personality leans toward peaceful, serene, and grounding:

- **Colors & Artwork:** Stick to neutral, soft tones – whites, creams, gentle pastels, and earthy hues. Artwork can be minimal, abstract, or soft landscapes that soothe the mind.
- **Plants & Nature:** Choose greenery in **terracotta, white, or ceramic pots** to create cohesiveness and a calming vibe. A few well-placed plants can bring life without clutter.
- **Textures & Comfort:** Layer cozy throws, soft rugs, and textured pillows to create a tactile sanctuary. Bedrooms, especially, should feel inviting, restful, and cocoon-like.
- **Room Harmony:** Keep energy consistent throughout your home. Even minimalistic homes benefit from repeating textures, colors, or shapes to maintain balance.

Practical Tips for Any Home Personality

- **Use What You Have:** Styling isn't about buying new things. Rearrange, repurpose, and highlight the treasures you already own. Your home will feel authentic and grounded.

- **Add a Statement Piece in Each Room:** Even a single item in a back corner – a vase, sculpture, or lamp – creates a sense of depth, intrigue, and energy.
- **Experiment with the Powder Room:** The main-floor powder room is a perfect place to take creative risks. Bold colors, dramatic wallpaper, or unique art here make a memorable statement without overwhelming your whole home.
- **Keep Bedrooms Cozy:** Prioritize comfort and rest. Soft bedding, calming colors, and minimal clutter support rejuvenation and better sleep.
- **Follow Your Intuition:** Your home is alive, and it will respond to your energy. Notice what feels right in each room and trust your instincts – styling should be playful and joyful, not stressful.

Styling your home is like giving it a voice. A vibrant, playful space sings with energy, while a calm, serene space hums with peace. By aligning your home's personality with your own, you create an environment that supports your energy, amplifies your intentions, and nourishes your soul every single day.

Allow this energy to spill into your daily life. Who are you? How do you want to express yourself? Me?

I'm a small town, country girl gone world traveler and my superpower is bringing space to life whether it is a 7-unit micro resort or an 1870s cabin on five acres. I am fueled by inspiration.

How would you describe yourself?

Is this who you are today? Or who you want to be 18 months from now? I invite you to really start moving towards your true, authentic self. Choose who you want to be and fill in the blanks. Or write your own statement in your own words. Keep this statement where you see it often. It creates miracles. It will move mountains. It will bring you what you desire and what you deserve. Bring this energy into your home, your work, your clothing, your hobbies. This is your lifestyle coming to life!

I'm a_____

gone_____.

And my superpower is:_____

_____.

.

Chapter 24

Up for Sale

Putting Your Magnetic Home on the Market

Most of us don't realize how much a home has influenced our life until we put it up for sale. Whether you are someone who has lived in your home for fifty years or someone who has moved every few years, selling a home can bring an entire range of emotions: it can bring joy and it can bring sadness.

Selling a home isn't just about listing it on a website or making cosmetic improvements. A truly magnetic home goes beyond paint colors and staging – it radiates energy that attracts the right buyers effortlessly. When your home is energetically aligned, it not only looks appealing, but it *feels* right, creating a lasting impression on everyone who enters.

Think of it this way: buyers don't just buy square footage or granite countertops – they buy how the space makes them feel. By consciously raising your home's vibration, you set the stage for a smooth sale, higher offers, and buyers who are aligned with the energy of your home. This goes for renters, too.

I was traveling a lot, Hurricanes Helene and Milton hit my area of St. Pete Beach, Florida hard. The entire area was devastated. I was in Colorado, and I woke up to hear a voice say,

"Put your home up for rent, NOW!" I listened to that voice and within three hours my home was listed. The only person I spoke to was an 87-year-old woman who had just lost her home of fifty years, and she was very interested in renting. She is my ideal renter and continues to love my condo.

I couldn't even imagine how that would feel to lose so much. When I got back to Florida, I put all the love and energy I could into my home intending that Joy would feel loved and at peace in her new condo. I gave her all the flexibility I could by offering her a trial run for three months and the option to stay for as long as she felt at home there. I even had a party for her so she could meet all her wonderful new neighbors.

She absolutely loves living there. And she blesses me, too, by giving me the option to be free to move about the world.

Clear Clutter and Stagnant Energy

Before anything else, remove clutter and stagnant energy from your home. This does several things:

- ✓ Opens up the flow of chi so buyers feel free and expansive.
- ✓ Sends a signal to the universe that you are ready for change and abundance.
- ✓ Makes rooms feel larger, brighter, and more welcoming.

Tips:

- ✓ Go room by room and ask: "Does this space feel expansive or weighed down?"
- ✓ Pass along items that no longer serve you to friends, family, or donation.
- ✓ Box up as many things you don't use as you can. Store them in one place in the garage or basement.
- ✓ For books, décor, and personal items, keep only those that elevate the space energetically.

Remember: a home that holds excess or heavy energy may unconsciously signal buyers that the home carries "baggage." Clear it, and you make room for positive intentions to flow in.

Raise the Vibration

Once your home is cleared, it's time to raise the energy so that it feels light, inviting, and alive. Here's how:

- ✓ **Lighting:** Open curtains, let natural light in, and add warm lamps to brighten corners.
- ✓ **Plants & Flowers:** Healthy plants signal growth, vitality, and life. Fresh flowers add movement and scent.
- ✓ **Scent:** Light a subtle candle, diffuse essential oils, or bake something simple to invoke feelings of comfort and home.
- ✓ **Sound:** Soft music tuned to 432 Hz or gentle Solfeggio frequencies can make rooms feel harmonious and calm.

You can even do a short space clearing ritual with a bell, incense, or prayer to uplift the entire home's vibration before listing. This aligns both you and your space with the energy of the right buyer.

Energetic Staging

Beyond aesthetics, think energetically about how each room should feel:

- ✓ **Entryway:** The first impression sets the tone. Keep it open, light, and welcoming. A healthy plant or cheerful artwork signals abundance and joy.
- ✓ **Living Spaces:** Arrange furniture in a way that encourages connection and flow. Avoid overcrowding – space should feel expansive, not cramped.
- ✓ **Kitchen:** The "stove of wealth" should be sparkling clean. Display fresh fruit or a vase of flowers to represent abundance.

✓ **Bedrooms:** Make these cozy, inviting, and restful. Soft textures, neutral colors, and tidy closets send a signal of comfort and peace.

✓ **Powder Room / Bathrooms:** Add a little "pop" here – a statement piece of art, a fragrant hand soap, or a decorative towel – to create memorable energy without overwhelming.

tip

Use statement pieces in the back corners to expand the feeling of space and draw the eye through the room. It's like giving buyers little "energy anchors" that subtly guide them through the home.

Depersonalize, And Keep Energy Alive

While buyers need to imagine themselves in the home, depersonalizing doesn't mean draining the energy:

✓ Remove family photos, personal collections, and overly specific décor.

✓ Keep art, colors, and objects that lift the vibration.

✓ Highlight spaces that feel joyful, open, and welcoming.

Think of your home as a **canvas of energy**: buyers should feel inspired, uplifted, and at ease.

Align Your Intention

Selling a home is a two-way flow of energy. Your intention sets the tone:

✓ Focus on the outcome you want: the right buyer, smooth process, and abundant sale.

✓ Avoid desperation or attachment to the outcome – let go of "how" it will happen.

✓ Affirm your intention daily: "I release my home to the perfect buyer who will love it, honor it, and enjoy its energy. The sale is easy, abundant, and harmonious."

This alignment sends ripples of energy out into the universe that attract buyers who resonate with your home's unique vibration.

Magical Touches

Here are some little extras that can make a big difference energetically:

- ✓ **Front Door Energy:** Sweep, polish, and add a welcoming mat or plant.
- ✓ **Energy Anchors:** Place a small crystal, candle, or decorative object in corners to subtly lift chi.
- ✓ **Music:** Light background music during showings to keep energy smooth.
- ✓ **Scent Memory:** A signature scent can linger in the buyer's subconscious, making your home unforgettable.

Trust the Flow

Once you've prepared your home energetically, trust the process:

- Your space has done its work.
- The right buyer is out there, resonating with the energy you've cultivated.
- Your role is to maintain alignment, keep your vibration high, and release attachment.

When your home is energetically aligned, selling it becomes more than a transaction – it's a magnetic experience. Buyers will feel it. They will connect. And the universe will reward your conscious effort.

Selling a home is a sacred dance between your intentions, your space, and the universe. By preparing your home energetically:

- ✓ You attract buyers who resonate with your space.

✓ You honor the energy of your home and the memories within.

✓ You maximize both the monetary and vibrational value of your property.

Your home has supported you. Now, let it support the next chapter for someone else – and for you.

Before & After Sale Magnetic Energy Checklist

Use this checklist to ensure your home is energetically aligned, welcoming, and ready to attract the perfect buyer.

Before Listing: Clearing & Uplifting Energy

Clutter Clear-Out

☐ Remove unnecessary items, old décor, and excess furniture.

☐ Pass along books, décor, or personal items that hold heavy energy.

Stagnant Energy Release

☐ Open windows and doors to let fresh air circulate.

☐ Use a bell, incense, or sage to clear stagnant energy from rooms, corners, and closets.

☐ Walk through each room with intention: "I release all that no longer serves this space."

Light & Vibe Check

☐ Replace burnt-out bulbs and maximize natural light.

☐ Ensure each room feels spacious, calm, and inviting.

☐ Play 432 Hz music or Solfeggio frequencies to raise vibration.

Statement & Anchor Pieces

- ☐ Add one eye-catching, uplifting piece in the back corner of each room.
- ☐ Plants, crystals, or artwork can act as energy anchors.

Bedroom Sanctuary

- ☐ Make beds cozy and inviting.
- ☐ Keep bedding fresh and neutral.
- ☐ Remove personal photos but keep energy positive.

Kitchen & Bathrooms

- ☐ Clean and declutter counters.
- ☐ Add fresh fruit, flowers, or decorative soaps.
- ☐ Ensure floors and fixtures are sparkling.

Entryway / Front Door

- ☐ Sweep and clear pathway.
- ☐ Add a welcoming mat or potted plant.
- ☐ Energy should feel open, light, and inviting.

Intentional Affirmations

- ☐ Daily: "My home attracts the perfect buyer who will honor its energy. The sale is smooth, abundant, and joyful."

After Cleaning & Styling: Energy Alignment

Flow Check

- ☐ Walk through each room. Ask: "Does this space feel expansive, inviting, and alive?"
- ☐ Make minor adjustments to furniture or décor as needed.

Room-Specific Energy Enhancements

- ☐ **Living Areas:** Encourage connection; add cozy seating and light accents.
- ☐ **Bedroom:** Calm, restful energy; soft textures and soothing colors.
- ☐ **Kitchen:** Abundance and nourishment; add vibrant or fresh touches.
- ☐ **Powder Room / Bathrooms:** Fun, memorable statement piece.

Scent & Sound

- ☐ Light a subtle candle or diffuse essential oils before showings.
- ☐ Play soft music tuned to 432 Hz or Solfeggio frequencies.

Front Door / First Impressions

- ☐ Ensure entrance is clean, vibrant, and inviting.
- ☐ A fresh-smelling, well-lit entryway sets the tone.

Energy Maintenance

- ☐ Daily: Invest 5–10 minutes walking through the home, clearing corners and refreshing energy.
- ☐ Keep intention clear and detached from outcome.

Final Touch

- ☐ Before showings: quick tidy, light a candle, play gentle music, and set intention:

"This home radiates love, abundance, and harmony. The right buyer is drawn effortlessly."

tip

Take a moment in each room to feel the energy shift. If a space feels heavy, add a plant, light, or uplifting object. Even small, mindful tweaks can make a huge difference in the flow of energy and the impression your home leaves on potential buyers.

A WORD FROM MY CLIENT

Buying & Selling Commercial Real Estate

Tonja has been my feng shui consultant since I got married in 2011. I believe that by following these feng shui principles, I was able to reach my goal of $10 Million in sales for my staffing business and was able to move into our dream family home. She has evaluated every house and every building I have moved my business to since. Following her feng shui and manifestation recommendations, I have been able to live a more harmonious, healthier and successful life. This year she visited a new building I bought for our staffing agency and helped me design the floor plan. We have now moved in and I love the layout. I am so grateful for all the help that Tonja has given me over the years, and I feel very blessed to know her.

Jessica C.
Commercial Property Investor
Arlington, Texas

My Deepest Gratitude

Thank you for bringing me along on your magical journey of creating your Magnetic Home. Manifesting Your Dream Life is not a finish line – it is a lifelong journey. It's an ongoing dance with the energy of the Universe, your inner self, and the spaces you inhabit. Every thought, every intention, and every action contributes to the life you are creating. And the beautiful truth is: the journey itself is just as magical as the destination.

Your home, your sanctuary, your sacred space is a mirror of your inner world. When you bring intention, love, and clarity into your environment, it amplifies your vibration and supports the life you deserve. But even as your home evolves, your growth is ongoing. New desires, new challenges, and new opportunities will arise – and your space can grow with you, continuing to reflect your highest self. It's an incredible experience to start manifesting so quickly that you start completing your bucket list faster than you can dream up what's next!

Remember that I am here for you if you get "stuck" or just need a friend to talk something through. And here are some tips to keep you going.

- ✓ **Remember to celebrate your wins**. Every positive shift – whether it's clearing clutter, welcoming a new energy flow, or affirming abundance – reinforces your power. Take a moment to appreciate the progress you make each day.

- ✓ **Stay Curious:** Explore new practices, experiment with colors, textures, sounds, and layouts in your home. Your curiosity fuels creativity and expansion. Children are great manifestors. Be child-like in your creations.

- ✓ **Trust the Process:** Sometimes, change is subtle. Sometimes, it's dramatic. Trust that every experience, every challenge, and every joy is guiding you closer to alignment with your soul's desires.

Most importantly, remember you have the power!!

The energy, wisdom, desire to create your dream life already exists within you. Your thoughts, your energy, and the vibrational alignment of your home are your tools. By combining intention with inspired action, by raising your vibration, and by honoring the spirit of all things around you, you are an active participant in the unfolding of your life.

Manifesting is not about luck, wishful thinking, or perfection, it's about alignment, authenticity, and consistent energetic practice. The Universe responds to the energy you emit. Keep your heart open, your intentions clear, and your space vibrant, and life will respond with abundance, joy, and opportunities that support your highest path.

Your life is a living canvas. Every day, every thought, and every choice adds a brushstroke. You have the power to consciously create a life of abundance, joy, and alignment. Use the energy of your home, your mind, and your heart to co-create with the Universe. The journey is ongoing, and the possibilities are infinite.

Thousands of big hugs in all your endeavors. I would love to hear about your successes and if you have any questions, please feel free to reach me. I'm only an email away!

With much love and gratitude,

Tonja

About the Author

One trip to a bookstore changed Tonja Waring's life forever. Eight months pregnant with her first child, Tonja wandered into the feng shui section of Barnes & Noble. As she flipped through the pages, the teachings felt deeply familiar; she was remembering rather than learning. It was this moment she realized she had been a feng shui master in a past life and that this ancient wisdom was woven into her soul.

Since that day, feng shui, manifesting, and working with energy have been the cornerstone of Tonja's life. She has studied with experts in many esoteric modalities as well as establishing her own modalities through spiritual guidance.

Known internationally as The Wise Mystic, she has been guiding people since 1995 how to design and live a life they are truly passionate about based on what they love, not who they've been. Blending ancient wisdom with modern practicality, Tonja helps people align their homes, hearts, and energy with their deepest desires.

Her passion for Manifesting Feng Shui has grown out of three decades of hands-on experience and discovery. Tonja has taught thousands through her books, courses, and private consultations, and has conducted hundreds of feng shui consultations for homes and businesses around the world. Her work reveals the profound connection between our mindset, the spaces we live in and the lives we create.

In *Magnetic Home*, Tonja shares a powerful truth: our homes are not just places we live, but sacred mirrors of our soul's journey. When we create intentional, high-vibrational spaces, we naturally magnetize health, wealth, joy, and harmony, and step into the life we were born to live.

Other Books by Tonja:

The Power of Manifesting
The Power of Affluence

Visit my website for lots of great
inspiration!
www.tonja.com

Questions? Reach out. I'm here for you.

Email: hello@tonja.com

WhatsApp: 1-972-632-6364

Cell: 1-972-632-6364

IG: @manifestingfengshui

FB facebook.com/tonja.waring.2025

Notes

Notes

Notes

Notes

Notes

www.ingramcontent.com/pod-product-compliance
Lightning Source LLC
Chambersburg PA
CBHW021503090426
42739CB00007B/441